Holiday Baking

GENERAL EDITOR
CHUCK WILLIAMS

RECIPES
JEANNE THIEL KELLEY

PHOTOGRAPHY
ALLAN ROSENBERG

TIME
LIFE
BOOKS

Time-Life Books is a division of
TIME LIFE INCORPORATED

President and CEO: John M. Fahey, Jr.
President, Time-Life Books: John D. Hall

TIME-LIFE CUSTOM PUBLISHING

Vice President and Publisher: Terry Newell
Sales Director: Frances C. Mangan
Editorial Director: Donia Steele

WILLIAMS-SONOMA
Founder/Vice-Chairman: Chuck Williams

WELDON OWEN INC.
President: John Owen
Publisher/Vice-President: Wendely Harvey
Associate Publisher: Laurie Wertz
Managing Editor: Lisa Chaney Atwood
Consulting Editor: Norman Kolpas
Copy Editor: Sharon Silva
Design: John Bull, The Book Design Company
Production Director: Stephanie Sherman
Production Editor: Janique Gascoigne
Co-Editions Director: Derek Barton
Co-Editions Production Manager (US): Tarji Mickelson
Food Photographer: Allan Rosenberg
Additional Food Photography: Allen V. Lott
Food Stylist: Heidi Gintner
Prop Stylist: Sandra Griswold
Food Stylist Assistant: Nette Scott
Food & Prop Assistant: Elizabeth C. Davis
Glossary Illustrations: Alice Harth

The Williams-Sonoma Kitchen Library
conceived and produced by Weldon Owen Inc.
814 Montgomery St., San Francisco, CA 94133

In collaboration with Williams-Sonoma
100 North Point, San Francisco, CA 94133

Production by Mandarin Offset, Hong Kong
Printed in China

A Note on Weights and Measures:
All recipes include customary U.S. and metric
measurements. Metric conversions are based on
a standard developed for these books and have
been rounded off. Actual weights may vary.

A Weldon Owen Production

Copyright © 1995 Weldon Owen Inc.
All rights reserved, including the right of
reproduction in whole or in part in any form.

Library of Congress
Cataloging-in-Publication Data:

Kelley, Jeanne Thiel.
   Holiday baking / general editor, Chuck Williams ;
recipes, Jeanne Thiel Kelley ; photography, Allan Rosenberg.
      p.   cm. — (Williams-Sonoma kitchen library)
   Includes index.
   ISBN 0-7835-0308-3
   1. Baking.   2. Holiday cookery.   I. Williams, Chuck.
II. Title.   III. Series.
TX765.K45   1995
641.8'15—dc20   94-48064
                                   CIP

Contents

CAKES & PASTRIES 15

BREADS & COFFEE CAKES 37

COOKIES 61

PIES & TARTS 85

INTRODUCTION

For me, the holidays have always been synonymous with baking. Batch after batch of butter cookies and gingerbread men. Mince pies and jam tarts cooling on the sideboard. Fruitcakes everywhere, to be given as gifts or shared when visitors stop by for coffee or tea. And, one of my personal favorites, a glorious steamed plum pudding as the grand finale to Christmas dinner.

The aim of this book is to share with you the myriad pleasures of festive baking. Its primary goal, however, is to show how easy it can be to make holiday cookies, pies, cakes, breads, coffee cakes and pastries in your own kitchen.

To that end, several introductory pages present a comprehensive survey of all the basic information you'll need to know, from selecting the right equipment to buttering and flouring a cake pan, from melting chocolate to preparing yeast-leavened breads, from topping a pie with a lattice crust to embellishing a cake with a decorative glaze. You'll also find basic recipes for pie or tart pastry and a range of fillings, frostings and icings. These fundamentals are followed by 45 recipes for holiday baked goods, divided into chapters by type: cakes and pastries, breads and coffee cakes, cookies, and pies and tarts.

As you look through this book, you'll quickly discover how widely varied the recipes are, embracing traditions from all over the world. You'll also soon realize that they don't confine themselves just to the so-called holiday season of autumn and early winter. There are romantic treats for Valentine's Day, celebrations of summer's ripe fruits and a wealth of baked goods that you can prepare to mark your own personal holidays—a birthday, an anniversary, a graduation.

I hope that, with the help and inspiration of the recipes contained in these pages, you'll find countless ways to make any day a holiday.

Chuck Williams

EQUIPMENT

Assembling an array of general-purpose and specialized tools for your holiday baking needs

The wide range of equipment on display here reflects the delightful diversity of holiday baked goods. A few basic pieces of equipment, such as some simple, sturdy baking sheets and cake pans, will enable you to make most of the recipes in this book.

Other recipes, however, require more specialized equipment, such as a decorative rolling pin to make German springerle or a heart-shaped cake pan. Although you might use these just once or twice a year, the pleasure such baked goods can bring more than compensates for the equipment's relatively minor expense.

1. Electric Mixer
Heavy-duty countertop mixer with stainless-steel bowl assists in mixing any dough or batter.

2. Mixer Attachments
The tree-shaped paddle attachment of an electric mixer is often used for creaming butter mixtures and smoothing out lumps without incorporating much air into batters. The dough hook kneads yeast-leavened doughs in less time than it takes to knead the same dough by hand.

3. Jelly-roll Pan
Large, shallow rectangular baking pan with rim (also known as Swiss-roll pan) produces cakes thin enough to be rolled up jelly-roll style.

4. Baking Sheet
Rimless baking sheets make removing cookies with a spatula easier. Dark, heavy-duty metal sheets conduct heat well for faster, more even browning.

5. Wire Rack
Sturdy, stainless-steel racks hold cookies, cakes and pastries for quick and even cooling after baking.

6. Assorted Utensils
Crockery jar holds sturdy rubber spatulas for folding, scraping and smoothing batters; wooden spoons and a wire whisk for stirring and mixing batters; pastry brushes for brushing glazes onto baked goods; a pastry wheel for decoratively cutting pastry dough.

7. Round Cake Pan
Choose a sturdy pan made of aluminum, stainless steel or tinned steel. The standard pan is about 9 inches (23 cm) in diameter and 1½ inches (4 cm) deep.

8. Springform Pan
Circular pan with high spring-clip sides that loosen easily for unmolding delicate cakes.

9. Bundt Pan
Decorative pan for baking traditional German coffee cakes includes tube to conduct heat to the center of the cake for more even baking. Stick-resistant lining simplifies unmolding the cake.

10. Rolling Pin
Select a sturdy hardwood dowel-type pin for best control when rolling out dough. To prevent warping, do not wash; wipe clean with a dry cloth.

11. Charlotte Mold
Traditional French bucket-shaped, tinned-steel mold, also ideal for baking cylindrical loaves such as Italian holiday panettone.

12. Pie Pan
Metal—preferably aluminum—conducts heat best for a crisp crust. Some are available with tiny holes in the pan bottom to ensure even browning of the crust.

13. Fine-mesh Sieve
For dusting the surface of finished baked goods with confectioners' (icing) sugar or cocoa.

14. Heart-shaped Cake Pan
Tinned-steel cake pan with 2-inch (5-cm) sides adds an expressive touch to cakes baked for heartfelt occasions.

15. Tube Pan
For baking angel's food and other delicate cake batters that require heat to be conducted to the center for even baking.

16. Pastry Bag and Tips
Plastic-lined cloth bag and stainless-steel tips enable easy, accurate piping of decorative icings. Choose larger bags, which are easier to fill and handle.

17. Nutmeg Grater
Rotary (pictured) or small, half-cylindrical graters, freshly grate the whole hard nutmeg pit.

18. Cookie Cutters
Sturdy tinned- or stainless-steel cutters provide a wide variety of attractive shapes to suit holiday themes.

19. Pot Holders
For safe removal of baking sheets and pans from the oven, choose heavy-duty quilted cotton pot holders and oven mitts with one side treated for fire resistance.

20. Tart and Tartlet Pans
Removable bottoms of standard 9-inch (23-cm) and individual 4-inch (10-cm) tart pans allow tarts to be unmolded, and fluted sides give pastry crust an attractive edge. Smaller tartlet tins in assorted sizes and shapes allow shaping and baking of individual and bite-sized pastries.

21. Springerle Rolling Pin
Traditional embossed German rolling pin for forming decorative holiday cookies.

22. Pastry Blender
For cutting butter or shortening into flour when making pastry dough by hand.

23. Pudding Mold
Tinned-steel mold with lid held in place by metal clips, for steaming traditional English-style holiday puddings.

Holiday Baking Essentials

Holiday baking presents the home cook with no special challenges, apart from the simple fact that, more than at any other time of year, you're likely to want to achieve perfectly beautiful results. The best way to ensure success is to follow the recipe directions exactly and pay attention to the basic skills demonstrated on these pages.

Beyond that, it is especially important to calibrate your oven by setting it to a common baking temperature and placing a good-quality oven thermometer inside on a middle shelf. When the oven is fully heated, compare its setting to the temperature registered on the thermometer. Take note of any difference between them and calculate it into the temperature at which you set the oven for any given recipe in this book.

Preparing the Pan

Instructions for preparing cake pans will vary from recipe to recipe, depending on the contents of the batter, how it is leavened and how much the cake will rise. The most common preparation consists of simply coating the inside of the pan with butter and flour to prevent the cake from sticking.

Dusting the pan with flour. Using your fingers or a paper towel, smear a thin, even coating of softened butter on the bottom and sides of the cake pan. Add a spoonful of flour to the pan, then tilt and shake the pan in all directions to coat the butter evenly with the flour. Tap out any excess flour.

Working with Egg Whites

Beaten to soft or stiff peaks and carefully folded together with other ingredients, egg whites lighten many cake and cookie batters. For perfect beating, start with clean, dry utensils.

Folding in beaten egg whites. Whether folding beaten egg whites into a batter, as shown here, or folding dry ingredients into the egg whites, use a large rubber spatula to combine the mixtures gently, maintaining maximum volume. Work in a circular motion, moving from the bottom of the bowl to the side and up over the top.

Melting Chocolate

Chocolate scorches easily when direct heat is applied. The gentle, indirect heat of a double boiler or a heatproof bowl set atop a pan of simmering water will ensure perfect melting.

Melting in a double boiler. Partially fill the bottom of a double boiler with water and bring to a low simmer. Put chocolate in the top pan and stir gently over the heat until the chocolate is fluid. Take care that the pan does not touch the water and that the water does not create steam.

MAKING ROLLED CAKES

A sheet cake baked in a jelly-roll (Swiss-roll) pan can be easily rolled up to form a festive mocha bûche de noël (recipe on page 20) or other rolled cake. Lining the pan with parchment paper makes the thin cake easier to handle.

Rolling up jelly-roll style.
Unmold the cake onto a large sheet of waxed paper dusted with confectioners' (icing) sugar. Peel off the parchment paper from the cake bottom and spread the cake evenly with filling. Then, starting at one long edge and using your hands, carefully roll up the cake to enclose the filling.

*Bittersweet Chocolate
Valentine Cake*

HOLIDAY DECORATING

The holidays call for a festive approach to decorating baked goods. Even a simply applied glaze or some carefully selected seasonal garnishes, such as sugared flowers, will add a spirit of celebration.

Piping a glaze.
Prepare a glaze or melted chocolate or ganache and spoon it into a small plastic bag. Seal the bag securely, snip off one corner and gently squeeze the bag while moving it to form a design of your choosing. Alternatively, use a pastry (piping) bag with a small, plain tip.

Drizzling a glaze.
Prepare a glaze or melt some chocolate and, using the tines of a fork or a small spoon, drizzle the glaze across the surface by waving the fork or spoon back and forth to form an abstract design.

Making sugared flowers.
Use only nontoxic, pesticide-free fresh flowers. Using a pastry brush, lightly brush each flower all over with egg white. Then, holding the flower over a bowl of granulated sugar, spoon the sugar over the flower until it is evenly coated. Let dry, petal side up, for about 20 minutes before using.

9

Making Yeast Breads

Making yeast-leavened breads with success takes some skill. But the homespun efforts involved in practicing that skill—the mixing and kneading of the dough and the patient waiting while it rises—bring baking devotees tremendous satisfaction. And the beautiful and delicious loaves that result more than reward the work.

The first major steps in making any yeast-leavened holiday bread—here, Dresden stöllen (recipe on page 39)—are to mix and knead the dough. Kneading—that is, the repeated folding, pressing and turning of the dough with your hands—develops the microscopic elastic network of gluten that traps the gas released by the yeast, causing the bread to rise and giving it a fine, evenly textured crumb. Punching down the risen dough allows it to rise a second time, further developing its texture and flavor.

The final step, of course, comes in baking the bread. As with any baking, you should take special care to calibrate your oven with a good-quality oven thermometer, to ensure that your holiday bread bakes at the temperature specified in its recipe.

2. *Letting the dough rise.* Gather the dough into a ball. Grease a large, clean bowl with butter or oil, place the dough in it and turn the dough ball to coat all surfaces. Cover with a clean kitchen towel and let stand in a warm, draft-free place until the dough rises to double its original volume.

3. *Punching down the dough.* Using the knuckles of your closed hand, punch down on the center of the dough to deflate it. Shape the dough or divide it into individual pieces, as specified in the recipe. Knead briefly, then cover with the towel and let rise again before baking.

1. *Kneading the dough.* After mixing the dough as directed in the recipe, turn it out onto a floured work surface. Using one hand, press the dough down and away from you, then fold it back onto itself, giving it a quarter turn. Repeat the kneading procedure until the dough feels smooth and elastic.

Dresden Stöllen

Pie or Tart Pastry

This pastry can be prepared in advance, tightly wrapped and stored for up to 4 days in the refrigerator or up to 2 weeks in the freezer. Allow the dough to soften slightly at room temperature before rolling it out.

2⅓ cups (12 oz/375 g) all-purpose (plain) flour
1 tablespoon sugar
1 teaspoon salt
½ teaspoon grated lemon zest
½ cup (4 oz/125 g) unsalted butter, chilled, cut into
 8 pieces
½ cup (4 oz/125 g) solid vegetable shortening, chilled
2 tablespoons fresh lemon juice
2–3 tablespoons cold water

In a large bowl, stir together the flour, sugar, salt and lemon zest. Add the butter and shortening and, using your fingertips or a pastry blender, blend the ingredients together until the mixture resembles coarse meal. Using a fork, stir in the lemon juice. Stirring gently with the fork, add enough of the water, 1 tablespoon at a time, for the mixture to come together in moist, rough clumps.
 Divide the dough in half. Gather each half into a ball, then flatten each ball into a smooth disk about 5 inches (13 cm) in diameter. Wrap each disk in plastic wrap and refrigerate for 1 hour before rolling out the pastry.

*Makes 2 disks, enough dough for two
9-inch (23-cm) pie crusts*

PASTRY TECHNIQUES

To ensure a beautiful crust every time you bake, always treat the pastry with care. Make sure that your work surface is lightly floured to prevent sticking. After you have placed the dough in the pan, repair any tears by moistening the torn edges with a little water and pressing them together; or use pastry scraps to fill any larger gaps.

Lining a pie pan.
On a lightly floured work surface, roll out the chilled pastry disk into a round slightly larger in diameter than the pie or tart pan. To transfer the pastry, loosely roll it up around the pin, then unroll it onto the pan and press gently into the bottom and sides.

Weaving a lattice crust.
On a lightly floured surface, roll out pastry into a round. Using a pastry wheel, cut into strips. Place a large sheet of waxed paper on the work surface and dust lightly with flour. Weave the strips on top of the waxed paper to form a lattice. Lift the paper and slide the lattice onto the pie filling.

Fluting the pastry rim.
After the lattice or top pastry are in place, trim off overhanging edges. Lightly moisten the edge of the bottom pastry and press gently on the strips or top pastry to seal with the bottom pastry. Using your thumb and forefingers, decoratively flute the edge.

Vanilla Pastry Cream

Here is a simple pastry cream that makes a delicious filling for cakes and tarts. You need to use whole milk for this recipe; low-fat or nonfat milk will not produce the desired rich flavor or texture.

⅔ cup (5 fl oz/160 ml) milk
1 piece vanilla bean, 2 inches (5 cm) long,
   split in half lengthwise
2 egg yolks
3 tablespoons sugar
1 tablespoon cornstarch (cornflour)

*I*n a small, heavy saucepan over high heat, combine the milk and vanilla bean and bring to a simmer. Meanwhile, in a bowl, whisk together the egg yolks, sugar and cornstarch until well blended.

When the milk reaches a simmer, remove it from the heat and gradually whisk the hot milk mixture into the yolk mixture. Return the mixture to the saucepan and place it over medium heat. Cook, whisking constantly, until the pastry cream thickens and boils, about 1 minute. Discard the vanilla bean and transfer the pastry cream to a small bowl. Use as directed in specific recipes.

Makes about 1 cup (8 fl oz/250 ml)

Vanilla Pastry Cream

Bittersweet Chocolate Ganache

This irresistible ganache has a variety of uses: it's a filling when chilled until thick and solid, an icing when cooled just until spreadable, and a glaze when warm.

½ cup (4 fl oz/125 ml) heavy (double) cream
2 tablespoons unsalted butter
1 tablespoon light corn syrup
6 oz (185 g) European bittersweet chocolate,
   finely chopped

*I*n a small, heavy saucepan over high heat, combine the cream, butter and corn syrup. Bring to a boil and remove from the heat.

Stir in the chocolate and then place over low heat. Whisk until the chocolate melts and the mixture is smooth, about 1 minute. Remove from the heat and use as directed in specific recipes.

Makes about 1 cup (8 fl oz/250 ml)

Bittersweet Chocolate Ganache

White Icing

Use this easy-to-make icing to decorate cookies, cakes and coffee cakes. Add enough milk to achieve the desired consistency: less milk yields a thick frosting appropriate for piping or spreading onto cookies; more milk results in a thin glaze perfect for drizzling over cakes and coffee cakes.

1 cup (4 oz/125 g) confectioners' (icing) sugar
¼ teaspoon vanilla extract (essence)
4–5 teaspoons milk

*I*n a small bowl, combine the confectioners' sugar and vanilla. Stir in enough of the milk to thin the icing to the desired consistency.

Makes about ½ cup (4 fl oz/125 ml)

White Icing

Buttercream Frosting

Buttercream Frosting

To turn this creamy, rich icing into coffee buttercream frosting, add 2 teaspoons instant espresso powder to the egg yolk mixture before heating. For orange buttercream frosting, use orange-flavored liqueur in place of the brandy and add 1 teaspoon grated orange zest with the vanilla extract.

4 egg yolks
⅓ cup (3 oz/90 g) sugar
2 tablespoons brandy
¾ cup (6 oz/185 g) unsalted butter, at room temperature
½ teaspoon vanilla extract (essence)

*I*n the top pan of a double boiler or a heatproof bowl placed over (not touching) simmering water, combine the egg yolks, sugar and brandy. Whisk until very thick and pale, about 4 minutes. Remove the pan or bowl from over the water and let cool to room temperature.

In a bowl, combine the butter and vanilla. Using an electric mixer set on medium-high speed, beat until very soft and fluffy, about 5 minutes. Gradually beat in the cooled egg yolk mixture. Let the mixture stand at room temperature, stirring occasionally, until spreadable, about 20 minutes.

Use immediately, or cover and refrigerate overnight or freeze for up to 1 month. Before using, let stand at room temperature until softened, then beat with an electric mixer set on high speed until smooth and fluffy.

*Makes about 1½ cups
(12 fl oz/375 ml)*

Chocolate-Almond Cheesecake

1 cup (3 oz/90 g) chocolate cookie crumbs

1 cup (4 oz/125 g) sliced (flaked) almonds

¼ cup (2 oz/60 g) unsalted butter, melted and cooled

4 tablespoons (2 oz/60 g) plus 1½ cups (12 oz/375 g) sugar

10 oz (315 g) European bittersweet chocolate, chopped, plus additional melted bittersweet chocolate for garnish (optional)

2 lb (1 kg) cream cheese, at room temperature

½ cup (1½ oz/45 g) unsweetened cocoa

4 eggs

½ cup (4 fl oz/125 ml) heavy (double) cream

1 tablespoon vanilla extract (essence)

1½ teaspoons almond extract (essence)

2 cups (16 fl oz/500 ml) sour cream

marzipan fruits, optional

Decorated with miniature marzipan fruits, this cake makes a lovely dessert for Christmas Eve. Look for the fruits in candy shops and well-stocked food stores during the holidays.

*P*osition a rack in the middle of an oven; preheat to 350°F (180°C).

In a bowl, mix together the cookie crumbs, almonds, butter and 1 tablespoon of the sugar. Press evenly over the bottom of a 10-inch (25-cm) springform pan. Bake until just golden, about 12 minutes. Let cool on a rack. Leave the oven set at 350°F (180°C).

In the top pan of a double boiler or a heatproof bowl placed over (not touching) simmering water, place the 10 oz (315 g) chocolate. Heat, stirring, until melted and smooth. Let cool. In a large bowl, using an electric mixer set on medium speed, beat together the cream cheese, the 1½ cups (12 oz/375 g) sugar and the cocoa until blended, about 3 minutes. Beat in the cooled chocolate. Add the eggs, one at a time, beating after each addition. Beat in the cream, vanilla and 1 teaspoon of the almond extract.

Pour the chocolate mixture over the cooled crust. Bake until puffy and gently set in the center, about 1 hour. Let cool on a rack until the cake deflates slightly, about 20 minutes. Leave the oven temperature set at 350°F (180°C).

Meanwhile, in a bowl, stir together the sour cream and the remaining 3 tablespoons sugar and ½ teaspoon almond extract. Spread over the settled cheesecake. Return to the oven and bake until just set, about 8 minutes. Let cool completely on a rack.

If desired, dip fork tines into melted chocolate and wave the fork back and forth over the cheesecake to create a zigzag pattern. Cover and refrigerate overnight.

If you like, just before serving, arrange marzipan fruits around the top of the cake.

Makes one 10-inch (25-cm) cake; serves 12–16

Devil's Food Cupcakes

2 medium-size beets
2 cups (10 oz/315 g) all-purpose
   (plain) flour
⅔ cup (2 oz/60 g) unsweetened cocoa
1 teaspoon baking soda (bicarbonate
   of soda)
½ teaspoon salt
¾ cup (6 oz/185 g) unsalted butter,
   at room temperature
1½ cups (12 oz/375 g) sugar
2 eggs
1 teaspoon vanilla extract (essence)
1 cup (8 fl oz/250 ml) hot water
buttercream frosting, at room
   temperature, or bittersweet chocolate
   ganache, warm (recipes on pages 12–13)

Beets give these cupcakes a nice, moist texture and a slightly reddish hue. For a festive touch, lightly sprinkle colored sugar crystals over the frosting.

*T*rim the stems from the beets, leaving ½ inch (12 mm) intact. Place the beets in a saucepan with water to cover, bring to a boil, reduce the heat to medium-low and simmer until tender, about 30 minutes. Drain and let cool. Peel the beets and finely grate. You should have about ¾ cup (5 oz/ 155 g). Set aside. Reserve any left over for another use.

Position racks in the middle of an oven and preheat to 350°F (180°C). Line 24 standard-sized muffin pan cups with fluted paper liners. In a bowl, sift together the flour, cocoa, baking soda and salt. In another bowl, using an electric mixer set on medium speed, beat together the butter and sugar until light and fluffy, about 4 minutes. Add the eggs, one at a time, beating well after each addition. Beat in the beets and vanilla. Reduce the speed to low and beat in the flour mixture in two batches alternately with the hot water, beginning and ending with the flour mixture.

Spoon the batter into the prepared cups, filling each about two-thirds full. Bake until a toothpick inserted into the center of a cupcake comes out clean, about 20 minutes. Remove from the oven and immediately invert onto a rack. Turn the cupcakes right-side up and let cool completely.

Using an icing spatula, frost the cooled cupcakes with buttercream or drizzle with warm ganache. Serve immediately, or store, loosely draped with plastic wrap, at room temperature for up to 1 day.

Makes 24 cupcakes

Passover Vanilla-Orange Sponge Cake

1½ cups (12 oz/375 g) sugar

1 piece vanilla bean, about 2 inches (5 cm) long

10 eggs, separated, at room temperature

½ cup (4 fl oz/125 ml) fresh orange juice

1 tablespoon grated orange zest

¼ teaspoon salt

¾ cup (4 oz/125 g) Passover cake meal

½ cup (2 oz/60 g) potato starch

Passover cake meal is a fine matzoh meal specifically formulated for cake baking. Look for it in kosher markets or well-stocked food stores. Serve the cake with a strawberry-orange compote, if you like.

*P*osition a rack in the middle of an oven and preheat to 325°F (165°C). In a food processor fitted with the metal blade, combine the sugar and vanilla bean and process until fine; set aside.

In a bowl, using an electric mixer set on high speed, beat the egg yolks until very thick and pale, about 4 minutes. Place the vanilla sugar in a sifter and gradually sift directly onto the yolks, discarding any large pieces of vanilla bean. Continue to beat until the mixture is thick and pale and tripled in volume, about 5 minutes. Gradually beat in the orange juice and zest.

In a clean bowl, using clean, dry beaters, beat the egg whites and salt until stiff but not dry; set aside. Combine the cake meal and potato starch in the sifter and sift the mixture directly onto the egg yolk mixture. Using a rubber spatula, fold in gently but thoroughly. Then fold in the egg whites, again working gently but thoroughly.

Spoon into a tube pan 10 inches (25 cm) in diameter and 4 inches (10 cm) deep. Bake until golden and the top springs back when gently touched, about 50 minutes. Invert the cake in its pan onto the neck of a bottle. Let cool completely.

To remove the cake from the pan, run a sharp knife around edges of the pan to loosen the cake, then invert onto a cake plate. Carefully lift off the pan. Serve immediately, or cover with a cake dome and store at cool room temperature for up to 8 hours.

Makes one 10-inch (25-cm) cake; serves 8

Mocha Bûche de Noël

6 eggs

¾ cup (6 oz/185 g) granulated sugar

1 teaspoon instant espresso powder

¾ cup (4 oz/125 g) all-purpose (plain) flour

2 tablespoons unsweetened cocoa

¼ teaspoon salt

2 tablespoons unsalted butter, melted and cooled

confectioners' (icing) sugar

coffee buttercream frosting (recipe on page 13)

bittersweet chocolate ganache (recipe on page 12)

Position a rack in the middle of an oven and preheat to 350°F (180°C). Butter a 10-by-15-by-1 inch (25-by-37.5-by-2.5-cm) jelly-roll (Swiss-roll) pan. Line the bottom with parchment paper. Butter and flour the paper and pan sides.

In a large, heatproof bowl, combine the eggs, granulated sugar and espresso powder. Place over (not touching) gently boiling water and whisk until just warm to the touch. Remove from the heat. Using an electric mixer set on high speed, beat until tripled in volume and soft peaks form, about 3 minutes. In a sifter, combine the flour, cocoa and salt. Sift directly onto the egg mixture. Using a rubber spatula, gently fold the mixtures together. Drizzle on the butter and fold it in.

Pour the batter into the prepared pan. Bake until a toothpick inserted into the center of the cake comes out clean, about 15 minutes. Transfer to a rack and let cool completely in the pan.

Place a large sheet of waxed paper on a work surface. Using a sifter or sieve, generously dust the paper with confectioners' sugar. Invert the jelly-roll pan onto the paper and lift off the pan. Peel off the parchment paper.

Spread the buttercream evenly over the cake. Beginning at a long side, roll up the cake jelly-roll style. Using a sharp knife, cut off the ends on the diagonal so that each piece is 1 inch (2.5 cm) on one side and 3 inches (7.5 cm) on the other. Place one piece, cut side to cake, on top of the cake toward one end. Place the other piece, cut side to cake, on the side of the cake toward the other end. The cake should resemble a log with cut limbs.

Stir the ganache until spreadable, then frost the cake, including all the ends. Using a fork, run the tines in circles on the ends and cut limbs of the log. Then run the tines the length of the log to simulate bark. Just before serving, sift confectioners' sugar over the log, to simulate snow. Slice crosswise to serve.

Serves 12

Cranberry-Orange Cheesecake

1 cup (4 oz/125 g) dried cranberries

2 cups (6 oz/185 g) graham cracker
crumbs

½ cup (4 oz/125 g) unsalted butter,
melted and cooled

1¼ cups (10 oz/310 g) plus 2 tablespoons sugar

2 lb (1 kg) cream cheese, at room
temperature

½ cup (4 fl oz/125 ml) thawed,
undiluted frozen orange juice
concentrate

1 tablespoon grated orange zest

2 tablespoons orange-flavored liqueur,
such as Grand Marnier

5 eggs

2 cups (16 fl oz/500 ml) sour cream

If you like, garnish this Thanksgiving cheesecake with orange slices.

Place the dried cranberries in a small, heavy saucepan and add water to cover. Place over low heat, cover and bring to a simmer. Cook the cranberries until soft and plump, about 4 minutes. Remove from the heat and let cool. Drain off any liquid.

Position a rack in the middle of an oven and preheat to 350°F (180°C). In a bowl, combine the crumbs, melted butter and ¼ cup (2 oz/60 g) of the sugar. Using a fork, stir to mix well. Press the crumb mixture over the bottom and 2 inches (5 cm) up the sides of a springform pan 10 inches (25 cm) in diameter and 3 inches (7.5 cm) deep. Bake until the crust is just golden, about 12 minutes. Transfer to a rack and let cool. Leave the oven set at 350°F (180°C).

In a bowl, using an electric mixer set on medium speed, beat together the cream cheese and 1 cup (8 oz/250 g) of the sugar until smooth. Beat in the orange juice concentrate, orange zest and liqueur until well mixed. Add the eggs, one at a time, beating well after each addition. Using a rubber spatula, fold in the drained cranberries. Spoon the cream cheese mixture into the cooled crust. Bake until the cheesecake is just set when the pan is gently shaken, about 1 hour. Transfer to a rack and let cool slightly. Leave the oven set at 350°F (180°C).

In a small bowl, stir together the sour cream and the remaining 2 tablespoons sugar. Pour over the cheesecake, covering evenly. Bake until the sour cream is set, about 8 minutes.

Transfer to a rack and let cool completely. Cover and refrigerate overnight. To serve, remove the pan sides, carefully slip the cake onto a serving plate and cut into wedges.

Makes one 10-inch (25-cm) cake; serves 12

Steamed Plum Pudding

1 cup (6 oz/185 g) pitted prunes

1 cup (8 fl oz/250 ml) water

3 eggs

½ cup (4 oz/125 g) unsalted butter, at
   room temperature

1¾ cups (14 oz/440 g) sugar

2 tablespoons brandy

2 teaspoons vanilla extract (essence)

2 cups (10 oz/315 g) all-purpose
   (plain) flour

2 teaspoons ground cinnamon

1½ teaspoons baking soda (bicarbonate
   of soda)

1 teaspoon ground allspice

¾ teaspoon salt

¼ teaspoon ground cloves

½ cup (3 oz/90 g) golden raisins
   (sultanas)

½ cup (3 oz/90 g) dark raisins

½ cup (2 oz/60 g) chopped walnuts

This steamed pudding is lighter and easier to make than the traditional Christmastime recipe. To reheat the pudding, return it to the mold and steam until just heated through. Serve with lightly whipped cream or hard sauce.

*B*utter the bottom and sides of a 2-qt (2-l) steamed pudding mold, then dust with sugar. Butter and sugar the lid as well. In a small, heavy saucepan over high heat, combine the prunes and water. Bring to a simmer, reduce the heat to medium-low, cover and simmer until the prunes are very soft, about 15 minutes. Transfer the prunes and liquid to a blender and let cool briefly. Add the eggs and purée until smooth. Set aside.

In a large bowl, using an electric mixer set on medium speed, beat together the butter and sugar until light and fluffy, about 4 minutes. Beat in the prune mixture, brandy and vanilla.

In a sifter, combine the flour, cinnamon, baking soda, allspice, salt and cloves. Sift directly onto the prune mixture. Reduce the mixer speed to low and beat until blended. Beat in the golden and dark raisins and walnuts.

Spoon the batter into the prepared mold and attach the lid. Fill the bottom chamber of a 2-chambered steamer or a deep soup pot with water and bring to a boil over medium-high heat. Place the pudding mold in the top chamber or on a steamer rack set over (not touching) the water. Cover and steam until a toothpick inserted near the center of the pudding comes out clean, about 2 hours. (Check the water level periodically, adding more boiling water as necessary to maintain its original level.)

Detach the mold lid and invert the pudding onto a serving plate. Lift off the mold. Serve warm or at room temperature.

Serves 8

Lemon-Blueberry Bundt Cake

3 cups (12 oz/375 g) cake (soft-wheat)
    flour
½ teaspoon baking soda (bicarbonate
    of soda)
½ teaspoon salt
¾ cup (6 oz/185 g) unsalted butter,
    at room temperature
1¾ cups (14 oz/440 g) sugar
2 tablespoons minced lemon zest
3 eggs
¼ cup (2 fl oz/60 ml) fresh lemon juice
¾ cup (6 fl oz/180 ml) and 2 table-
    spoons buttermilk
¾ cup (3 oz/90 g) dried blueberries

FOR THE GLAZE:
¼ cup (2 oz/60 g) sugar
¼ cup (2 fl oz/60 ml) fresh lemon juice
2 tablespoons unsalted butter

If possible, use Meyer lemons for this summertime cake to give it a particularly pleasant sweet-tart flavor. The cake is the perfect choice to pack for a summer holiday picnic. If you like, place fresh blueberries in the center and lemon leaves and paper-thin lemon slices around the sides.

Position a rack in the middle of an oven; preheat to 350°F (180°C). Butter and flour a 10-inch (25-cm) bundt pan.

In a bowl, sift together the flour, baking soda and salt; set aside. In another bowl, using an electric mixer set on medium speed, beat together the butter, sugar and lemon zest until light and fluffy, about 4 minutes. Add the eggs, one at a time, beating well after each addition. Beat in the lemon juice. Reduce the speed to low and beat in the flour mixture in two batches alternately with the buttermilk, beginning and ending with the flour mixture. Stir in the dried blueberries.

Spoon the batter into the prepared pan. Bake until a toothpick inserted near the center of the cake comes out clean, about 55 minutes. Transfer the pan to a rack and let cool slightly.

To make the glaze, in a small saucepan over high heat, combine the sugar, lemon juice and butter. Bring to a boil, stirring to dissolve the sugar, then boil the mixture until syrupy, about 5 minutes.

Brush some of the glaze over the surface of the warm cake. Invert the cake onto a serving plate and carefully lift off the pan. Drizzle the cake with the remaining glaze. Let cool completely before serving.

Makes one 10-inch (25-cm) cake; serves 12

Dried Fruit and Nut Fruitcake

1 cup (6 oz/185 g) chopped dried pears

1 cup (6 oz/185 g) chopped dried
apricots

1 cup (6 oz/185 g) chopped dried
pitted prunes

½ cup (3 oz/90 g) dark raisins

½ cup (3 oz/90 g) golden raisins
(sultanas)

½ cup (2 oz/60 g) dried pitted sour
cherries

½ cup (2½ oz/75 g) pitted dates,
chopped

3 tablespoons finely chopped candied
orange peel

2 tablespoons finely chopped
crystallized ginger

½ cup (4 fl oz/125 ml) plus 3 tablespoons brandy

1½ cups (12 oz/375 g) unsalted butter,
at room temperature

2½ cups (1¼ lb/625 g) sugar

8 eggs, at room temperature

1 tablespoon vanilla extract (essence)

½ teaspoon salt

3 cups (9 oz/280 g) cake (soft-wheat)
flour, sifted before measuring

2 cups (8–10 oz/250–315 g) nuts, such
as walnuts, pecans, hazelnuts (filberts)
or almonds, toasted (see glossary,
page 106), cooled and chopped

This cake does not call for the traditional candied fruits that make most fruitcakes taste old-fashioned. Wrapped in plastic wrap, it can be stored in a cool place for several days.

*I*n a bowl, combine the pears, apricots, prunes, dark and golden raisins, cherries, dates, orange peel and ginger. Pour the ½ cup (4 fl oz/125 ml) brandy over the top. Let stand for at least 4 hours or as long as overnight at room temperature, stirring occasionally.

Position a rack in the middle of an oven and preheat to 325°F (165°C). Butter a tube pan 10 inches (25 cm) in diameter and 4¼ inches (10.5 cm) deep. Line the bottom of the pan with parchment paper or waxed paper cut to fit precisely. Butter the paper, then flour the paper and pan sides.

In a large bowl, using an electric mixer set on medium speed, beat the butter until light and fluffy, about 7 minutes. Add the sugar and continue beating until once again fluffy, about 4 minutes. Beat in the eggs, one at a time, beating well after each addition. Then beat in the vanilla and salt. Reduce the speed to low and beat in the flour. Using a wooden spoon, fold in the nuts and the brandy-fruit mixture until fully incorporated.

Spoon the batter into the prepared pan. Using the back of a wooden spoon, spread the batter evenly and smooth the top. Bake until a toothpick inserted near the center of the cake comes out clean, about 1 hour and 50 minutes. Transfer to a rack. Brush 1 tablespoon of the remaining brandy over the cake. Let cool in the pan for 5 minutes.

Invert the cake onto the rack; carefully lift off the pan and then peel off the paper. Brush the remaining 2 tablespoons brandy over the top and sides. Let cool completely before serving.

Makes one 10-inch (25-cm) cake; serves 12–20

Bittersweet Chocolate Valentine Cake

8 oz (250 g) European bittersweet
  chocolate
1 cup (8 oz/250 g) unsalted butter
5 eggs
1⅓ cups (11 oz/330 g) sugar
2 tablespoons all-purpose (plain) flour
1 tablespoon vanilla extract (essence)
¼ teaspoon salt
bittersweet chocolate ganache, warm
  (recipe on page 12)
2 oz (60 g) European white chocolate,
  melted (see glossary, page 104), optional

If your loved one is a chocolate addict, bake this for Valentine's Day. The cake can be sprinkled with chocolate curls (see glossary, page 104) or piped with melted white chocolate.

Position a rack in the middle of an oven and preheat to 325°F (165°C). Butter a heart-shaped cake pan 9 inches (23 cm) in diameter and 3 inches (7.5 cm) deep. Line the bottom of the pan with parchment paper cut to fit precisely. Butter the paper, then flour the paper and pan sides.

In a medium-sized, heavy saucepan over medium-low heat, combine the bittersweet chocolate and butter. Stir until melted and smooth, about 2 minutes. Remove from the heat and let cool slightly. In a large bowl, whisk together the eggs and sugar until blended. Whisk in the chocolate mixture, then stir in the flour, vanilla and salt until combined.

Pour the batter into the prepared pan. Bake until the cake is set and slightly puffed in the center, about 1 hour and 10 minutes. Transfer to a rack and let cool until warm. Invert onto a serving plate. Carefully lift off the pan and peel off the paper. Let cool completely.

Tuck strips of waxed paper under the edges of the cake. Pour the warm ganache over the top and, using an icing spatula, coax it down the sides. When the glaze stops dripping, remove the paper strips. Let cool and then chill until set, about 1 hour.

If using the white chocolate, spoon it into a small pastry bag fitted with a plain tip (or a small plastic bag with a corner snipped off) and pipe decoratively on top. Chill overnight before serving.

Makes one 9-inch (23-cm) cake; serves 8

Galette des Rois

⅔ cup (4 oz/125 g) blanched almonds, toasted (see glossary, page 106) and cooled

⅓ cup (1½ oz/45 g) confectioners' (icing) sugar

1 tablespoon cornstarch (cornflour)

2 eggs

1 tablespoon dark rum

¼ teaspoon almond extract (essence)

vanilla pastry cream, cooled to room temperature (recipe on page 12)

6 tablespoons (3 oz/90 g) unsalted butter, at room temperature

1 package (17¼ oz/537 g) frozen puff pastry sheets (2 sheets), thawed at room temperature

1 dried bean or a tiny porcelain figure

1 tablespoon milk

This cake, which literally translates as "kings' cake," is eaten in France on Twelfth Night, the eve of Epiphany. The bean or porcelain token hidden in the center is believed to bring good fortune to the person who finds it. Make sure you warn all who sample the cake about the surprise inside before they take a bite.

*P*osition a rack in the middle of an oven and preheat to 400°F (200°C).

In a food processor fitted with the metal blade, process the almonds, confectioners' sugar and cornstarch until the nuts are finely ground. Add 1 of the eggs, the rum and almond extract and use on-off pulses until blended. Add the pastry cream and process just until blended. With the motor running, add the butter, 1 tablespoon at a time, and process until smooth.

On a lightly floured work surface, roll out each puff pastry sheet into a 12-inch (30-cm) square. Using a piece of waxed paper cut to size as a guide, cut out a round 11 inches (28 cm) in diameter from each square. Discard the pastry scraps.

Transfer 1 pastry round to a baking sheet. Spread the almond filling evenly over the round, leaving a 1-inch (2.5-cm) border uncovered around the edges. Place the dried bean or porcelain figure atop the filling. In a small bowl, whisk together the remaining egg and the milk. Brush some of the mixture on the uncovered border. Place the other pastry round on top and press the edges together to seal. Brush the top with the remaining mixture. Using a long, sharp knife, score the top with a diamond pattern; be careful not to cut through to the filling.

Bake until the crust is golden brown, about 35 minutes. Transfer to a rack and let cool completely. To serve, carefully slip the cake onto a serving plate and cut into wedges.

Makes one 11-inch (28-cm) cake; serves 12

Pumpkin-Spice Layer Cake

1 can (1 lb/500 g) pumpkin purée

¾ cup (6 fl oz/180 ml) buttermilk

4 eggs

2 cups (16 oz/500 g) sugar

¾ cup (6 fl oz/180 ml) vegetable oil

1 teaspoon vanilla extract (essence)

3 cups (15 oz/470 g) all-purpose (plain) flour

2 teaspoons baking soda (bicarbonate of soda)

2 teaspoons ground cinnamon

1 teaspoon ground ginger

1 teaspoon salt

½ cup (3 oz/90 g) dried currants

¾ lb (375 g) cream cheese, at room temperature

3 cups (24 fl oz/750 ml) orange buttercream frosting, at room temperature *(recipe on page 13)*

Here is a delicious alternative to pumpkin pie for Thanksgiving dessert. Orange zest curls make an attractive garnish. To make them, use a zester to cut the zest into thin strips.

*P*osition racks in the middle of an oven and preheat to 350°F (180°C). Butter and flour 3 cake pans each 9 inches (23 cm) in diameter. In a large bowl, using an electric mixer set on medium speed, beat together the pumpkin purée and buttermilk until blended. Beat in the eggs, sugar, oil and vanilla.

In a sifter, combine the flour, baking soda, cinnamon, ginger and salt and sift the mixture directly onto the batter. Reduce the mixer speed to low and beat in the flour mixture, stopping occasionally to scrape down the sides, just until combined. Fold in the currants.

Divide the batter among the prepared pans. Bake until a tooth-pick inserted into the center of each cake comes out clean, about 25 minutes. Transfer to racks to cool for 10 minutes. Invert the cakes onto the racks, lift off the pans and let cool completely.

In a bowl, using the electric mixer set on medium-high speed, beat the cream cheese until very light and fluffy, about 4 minutes. Gradually beat in the buttercream frosting until well blended.

Place a cake layer on a cake plate. Using an icing spatula, spread the top with about ¾ cup (6 fl oz/185 ml) of the frosting. Top with a second cake layer and spread it with about ¾ cup (6 fl oz/185 ml) of the remaining frosting. Place the final cake layer on top. Spread the top and sides of the cake decoratively with the remaining frosting.

Serve immediately, or cover with a cake dome and store overnight at cool room temperature.

Makes one 9-inch (23-cm) cake; serves 8

Dresden Stöllen with Cranberries

½ cup (2 oz/60 g) dried cranberries

½ cup (3 oz/90 g) currants

⅓ cup (2 oz/60 g) diced citron

⅓ cup (2 oz/60 g) diced candied
  orange peel

¼ cup (2 fl oz/60 ml) brandy

¼ cup (2 fl oz/60 ml) warm water
  (120°F/49°C)

1 tablespoon active dry yeast

1 cup (8 fl oz/250 ml) milk, warmed

¾ cup (6 oz/185 g) unsalted butter,
  melted and cooled

½ cup (4 oz/125 g) granulated sugar

1 teaspoon salt

3 eggs

1 teaspoon almond extract (essence)

¾ cup (4 oz/125 g) almonds, toasted
  (*see glossary, page 106*), cooled and
  chopped

about 5½ cups (27½ oz/855 g) all-
  purpose (plain) flour

7 oz (220 g) marzipan

confectioners' (icing) sugar

*I*n a small bowl, combine the cranberries, currants, citron, orange peel and brandy. Cover and let stand overnight at room temperature.

Pour the warm water into a large bowl. Sprinkle the yeast over the top and let stand until dissolved, about 1 minute. Stir in the milk, melted butter, granulated sugar and salt. Whisk in the eggs and almond extract, then mix in the almonds and fruit mixture. Using a wooden spoon, gradually beat in about 4½ cups (22½ oz/705 g) flour to make a semisoft dough.

Transfer the dough to a floured work surface and knead, adding about 1 cup (5 oz/155 g) more flour as needed to prevent sticking, until smooth and elastic, about 5 minutes. Gather the dough into a ball, place in a bowl greased with butter, turn to coat with the butter and cover the bowl with a clean kitchen towel. Place in a warm, draft-free area until the dough is doubled in volume, about 2 hours.

Punch down the dough and transfer to a lightly floured work surface. Knead until smooth, about 3 minutes. Divide into 3 equal portions. Roll out each portion into a round ¾ inch (2 cm) thick. Pinch off bits of the marzipan and arrange evenly on the dough rounds. Roll up each round jelly-roll style. Grease 1 or 2 baking sheets with butter and place the rolls, seam side down, on the sheet(s). Cover with the kitchen towel and let rise in a warm, draft-free area until doubled in volume, about 45 minutes.

Meanwhile, position a rack in the middle of an oven and pre-heat to 375°F (190°C). Bake until the loaves are golden brown and sound hollow when thumped on the bottom, about 45 minutes. Transfer to a rack. Using a fine-mesh sieve, dust the hot loaves with confectioners' sugar. Let cool completely and again dust with confectioners' sugar before serving. Serve immediately, or wrap airtight and store at cool room temperature for 3 days.

Makes 3 loaves

Golden Panettone

1 cup (6 oz/185 g) golden raisins
   (sultanas)

½ cup (4 fl oz/125 ml) dry Marsala wine

4½ cups (22½ oz/705 g) all-purpose
   (plain) flour

½ cup (4 oz/125 g) sugar

1 tablespoon active dry yeast

1 teaspoon salt

1 cup (8 fl oz/250 ml) plus 1 tablespoon
   milk

½ cup (4 oz/125 g) unsalted butter

4 eggs

¾ cup (4 oz/125 g) pine nuts, lightly
   toasted (*see glossary, page 106*)

2 teaspoons grated orange zest

*I*n a small, heavy saucepan, combine the raisins and Marsala. Bring to a boil. Remove from the heat, cover and let stand overnight at room temperature.

In the bowl of a heavy-duty mixer fitted with the dough hook, combine 1½ cups (7½ oz/235 g) of the flour, the sugar, yeast and salt. In a small saucepan over low heat, combine the 1 cup (8 fl oz/250 ml) milk and butter and stir until the butter melts and the mixture is 125°F (52°C). Add the milk mixture to the flour mixture and beat on medium speed until well mixed. Beat in 3 of the eggs, then stir in the reserved raisins and Marsala, pine nuts and orange zest. Beat in the remaining 3 cups (15 oz/470 g) flour to make a soft dough.

Place the dough in a large bowl greased with butter. Cover with a kitchen towel and place in a warm, draft-free area until doubled in volume, about 2 hours.

Stir down the dough to remove the air pockets. Generously butter two 7-inch (18-cm) charlotte molds or two 1-lb (500-g) coffee cans with the tops removed. Line the bottoms with parchment paper. Butter the paper. Divide the dough evenly between the molds. Cover with the towel and let rise in a warm, draft-free area until doubled in volume, about 1 hour.

Position a rack in the middle of an oven and preheat to 375°F (190°C). In a small bowl, beat the remaining egg with the remaining 1 tablespoon milk. Brush evenly over the tops of the loaves. Bake until golden brown and a toothpick inserted near the center comes out clean, about 45 minutes. Transfer to a rack and let cool slightly. Then invert onto the rack, lift off the pans and peel off the paper. Turn right side up; let cool completely.

Makes 2 loaves

New Mexico Pueblo Bread

about 5 cups (25 oz/780 g) all-purpose
    (plain) flour
8 tablespoons (4 oz/125 g) unsalted
    butter, melted and cooled
3 tablespoons sugar
1 tablespoon active dry yeast
2 teaspoons salt
1½ cups (12 fl oz/375 ml) warm water
    (125°F/52°C)

New Mexico's Pueblo Indians bake these crusty loaves for festivals and holy days.

In the bowl of a heavy-duty mixer fitted with the dough hook, combine 1½ cups (7½ oz/235 g) of the flour, 2 tablespoons of the butter, the sugar, yeast and salt. Add the water and beat on medium-high speed until well mixed. Beat in 3–3½ cups (15–17½ oz/470–545 g) more flour to make a dough that is semisoft and no longer sticky. Or, to make the dough by hand, combine the ingredients as directed in a bowl and beat with a wooden spoon until the dough pulls away from the sides of the bowl.

Transfer to a floured work surface and knead, adding flour as needed to prevent sticking, until smooth and elastic, about 5 minutes. Gather the dough into a ball and place in a large bowl greased with 2 tablespoons of the butter. Turn to coat with the butter and cover the bowl with a clean kitchen towel. Place in a warm, draft-free area until doubled in volume, about 2 hours.

Punch down the dough and transfer to a lightly floured work surface. Knead until smooth, about 3 minutes. Divide the dough in half. Roll out each half into a round 8 inches (20 cm) in diameter. Brush each round with 2 tablespoons of the butter. Fold each round in half and press gently to close. Butter a baking sheet and place the loaves on it. Using a sharp knife, make 2 equidistant cuts crosswise in each loaf, cutting only two-thirds of the way through. Cover with the kitchen towel and let rise in a warm, draft-free area until doubled in volume, about 1 hour.

Meanwhile, position a rack in the middle of an oven and preheat to 375°F (190°C). Bake until the loaves are golden brown and sound hollow when thumped on the bottom, about 45 minutes. Let cool briefly on a rack, then pull apart at each section to serve.

Makes 2 loaves

Pear Kuchen

½ cup (4 oz/125 g) unsalted butter,
  at room temperature
½ cup (4 oz/125 g) plus 2 tablespoons
  sugar
1 tube (7 oz/220 g) almond paste
4 eggs, at room temperature
1 cup (5 oz/155 g) all-purpose
  (plain) flour
¼ teaspoon salt
4 large, firm yet ripe pears, peeled,
  halved, cored and cut into eighths
freshly grated nutmeg

Delicious fruit kuchen, the traditional German coffee cake, is perfect for serving at a brunch held on any autumn or winter holiday. During the summertime, substitute 8 large, red plums, halved, pitted and sliced, for the pears, and cinnamon for the nutmeg.

*P*osition a rack in the middle of an oven and preheat to 350°F (180°C). Butter a 9-by-12-inch (23-by-30-cm) baking dish.

In a bowl, using an electric mixer set on medium speed, beat together the butter and the ½ cup (4 oz/125 g) sugar until light and fluffy, about 4 minutes. Gradually beat in the almond paste. Add the eggs, one at a time, beating well after each addition. Continue beating until the mixture is light, about 3 minutes. Reduce the speed to low and beat in the flour and salt until well blended.

Spoon the batter into the prepared baking dish, spreading it evenly. Arrange the pear wedges in attractive rows over the surface, poking them gently into the batter. Sprinkle the pears with the remaining 2 tablespoons sugar and a light dusting of nutmeg. Bake until the pears are tender when pierced with a knife and the cake is golden brown, about 55 minutes.

Transfer to a rack and let cool slightly. Cut into squares to serve.

Makes one 9-by-12-inch (23-by-30-cm) cake; serves 12

Cherries and Cream Sweetheart Scones

2 cups (10 oz/315 g) plus 2 tablespoons all-purpose (plain) flour

⅓ cup (3 oz/90 g) plus 2 tablespoons sugar

1 tablespoon baking powder

½ teaspoon salt

6 tablespoons (3 oz/90 g) chilled unsalted butter, cut into 12 pieces

⅔ cup (3 oz/90 g) dried pitted sour cherries

1 cup (8 fl oz/250 ml) heavy (double) cream

Laced with dried cherries, these rich, heart-shaped scones are great for Valentine's Day breakfast or an afternoon tea. Serve with Devonshire cream. They are best enjoyed on the same day they are made.

*P*osition a rack in the middle of an oven and preheat to 400°F (200°C).

In a large bowl, combine the 2 cups (10 oz/315 g) flour, the ⅓ cup (3 oz/90 g) sugar, the baking powder and salt. Add the butter and, using your fingertips or a pastry blender, blend the ingredients together until the mixture resembles coarse meal. Using a fork, stir in the cherries and then the cream to form a soft dough. Let stand for 2 minutes.

Transfer the dough to a lightly floured surface. Sprinkle the top of the dough with the remaining 2 tablespoons flour. Using your fingertips, gently press out the dough into a round ½ inch (12 mm) thick. Using a floured heart-shaped cookie cutter 3 inches (7.5 cm) in diameter, cut out the scones. Transfer them to ungreased baking sheets, spacing them about 2 inches (5 cm) apart. Gather up the dough scraps, press out into a round ½ inch (12 mm) thick and cut out as many more scones as possible. Transfer to the baking sheets. Sprinkle the scones evenly with the remaining 2 tablespoons sugar.

Bake until golden brown, about 15 minutes. Remove from the oven and serve warm, or transfer to a rack, let cool and serve at room temperature.

Makes about 12 scones

Hot Cross Buns

¼ cup (2 fl oz/60 ml) lukewarm water
  (120°F/49°C)

1 tablespoon active dry yeast

½ cup (4 fl oz/125 ml) milk, warmed

6 tablespoons (3 oz/90 g) unsalted
  butter, melted and cooled

¼ cup (2 oz/60 g) sugar

1 whole egg, plus 1 egg yolk

2 teaspoons grated lemon zest

1 teaspoon freshly grated nutmeg

½ teaspoon salt

about 3½ cups (17½ oz/545 g)
  all-purpose (plain) flour

1 cup (6 oz/185 g) chopped raisins

white icing (recipe on page 13)

Hot cross buns have long been an Easter tradition in Britain. Leftover buns can be stored in an airtight container for up to 2 days.

*P*our the lukewarm water into a large bowl. Sprinkle the yeast over the top and let stand until dissolved, about 1 minute. Stir in the milk, 4 tablespoons (2 fl oz/60 ml) of the melted butter and the sugar. Whisk in the whole egg and egg yolk until mixed. Add the lemon zest, nutmeg and salt and stir well, then stir in 1½ cups (7½ oz/235 g) of the flour and the raisins. Using a wooden spoon, beat in about 1 cup (5 oz/155 g) more flour to make a dough that is semisoft and no longer sticky.

Transfer the dough to a floured work surface and knead, adding flour as needed to prevent sticking, until smooth and elastic, about 5 minutes. Gather the dough into a ball, place in a large bowl greased with butter, turn to coat with the butter and cover the bowl with a clean kitchen towel. Place in a warm, draft-free area until the dough doubles in volume, about 1½ hours.

Punch down the dough and transfer to a lightly floured work surface. Knead until smooth, about 3 minutes. Divide the dough into 12 equal portions and form each portion into a ball. Grease a baking sheet with butter and place the balls well apart on the sheet. Cover with the kitchen towel and let rise in a warm, draft-free area until doubled in volume, about 45 minutes.

Meanwhile, position a rack in the middle of an oven and pre-heat to 375°F (190°C). Using a sharp knife, cut a cross about ½ inch (12 mm) deep in the top of each bun. Brush the remaining 2 tablespoons melted butter evenly over the tops. Bake until the buns are golden brown and sound hollow when thumped on the bottoms, about 25 minutes. Let cool completely on a rack, then, using a spoon, fill each cross with the icing.

Makes 12 buns

Festive Challah

about 5 cups (25 oz/780 g) all-purpose
   (plain) flour
¼ cup (2 oz/60 g) sugar
1 tablespoon active dry yeast
1 teaspoon salt
⅛ teaspoon powdered saffron
1¼ cups (10 fl oz/315 ml) warm water
   (125°F/52°C)
6 tablespoons (3 oz/90 g) unsalted
   butter, at room temperature
3 eggs
1 tablespoon milk
1 tablespoon sesame seeds

*Challah is the traditional Jewish egg bread served on the Sabbath.
Here, the addition of saffron gives it a deeper golden hue.*

In the bowl of a heavy-duty mixer fitted with the dough hook,
combine 1½ cups (7½ oz/235 g) of the flour, the sugar, yeast,
salt and saffron. Add the water and beat on medium-high speed
until well mixed. Beat in the butter and 2 of the eggs. Then beat
in about 3 cups (15 oz/470 g) more flour to make a dough that
is semisoft and no longer sticky. Or, to make the dough by
hand, combine the ingredients as directed in a bowl and beat
with a wooden spoon until the dough pulls away from the sides.

Transfer the dough to a floured work surface and knead,
adding flour as needed to prevent sticking, until smooth and
elastic, about 5 minutes. Gather the dough into a ball, place in a
large bowl greased with butter, turn to coat with the butter and
cover the bowl with a clean kitchen towel. Place in a warm,
draft-free area until doubled in volume, about 1½ hours.

Punch down the dough and transfer to a lightly floured work
surface. Knead until smooth, about 3 minutes. Divide the dough
into 3 equal portions. Using your palms, roll each portion into a
rope 20 inches (50 cm) long. Butter a baking sheet. Braid the
ropes together and transfer the braid to the baking sheet, tucking
the ends under. Cover with the kitchen towel and let rise in a
warm, draft-free area until doubled in volume, about 1 hour.

Meanwhile, position a rack in the middle of an oven and
preheat to 350°F (180°C). In a small bowl, beat the remaining
egg with the milk until blended. Brush evenly over the braid.
Sprinkle with the sesame seeds. Bake until the bread is golden
brown and sounds hollow when thumped on the bottom, about
55 minutes. Let cool on a rack.

Makes 1 large loaf

Chocolate Bread

½ cup (4 fl oz/125 ml) warm water
  (120°F/49°C)
1 tablespoon active dry yeast
⅓ cup (3 oz/90 g) sugar
1½ teaspoons salt
4 eggs
¾ cup (6 oz/185 g) unsalted butter,
  melted and cooled
3 tablespoons unsweetened cocoa
3⅔ cups (19 oz/590 g) all-purpose
  (plain) flour
8 oz (250 g) bittersweet chocolate,
  coarsely chopped
white icing *(recipe on page 13)*

Here is a rich loaf that is a welcome addition to any holiday break-fast, especially when chocolate lovers are seated around the table. It is best eaten on the day it's made.

*P*our the warm water into a large bowl. Sprinkle the yeast over the top and let stand until the yeast dissolves, about 1 minute. Using a wire whisk, stir in the sugar and salt. Whisk in the eggs and butter until well mixed. Using a wooden spoon, beat in the cocoa and then the flour to make a soft dough.

Gather the dough into a ball, place in a large bowl greased with butter, turn to coat with the butter and cover the bowl with a clean kitchen towel. Place in a warm, draft-free area until the dough is doubled in volume, about 1½ hours.

Using a wooden spoon, stir the chocolate into the dough, removing any air pockets at the same time. Transfer the dough to a lightly floured work surface and knead briefly until the chocolate is incorporated and the dough is smooth. Divide the dough in half and form each half into a rectangular loaf, tucking under the ends. Generously butter two 4-by-8-inch (10-by-20-cm) loaf pans. Place the loaves in the prepared pans. Cover with the kitchen towel and let rise in a warm, draft-free area until doubled in volume, about 1 hour.

Meanwhile, position a rack in the middle of an oven and preheat to 375°F (190°C). Bake until the breads sound hollow when thumped on the bottom, about 40 minutes. Immediately turn out the loaves onto a rack.

While the loaves are still warm, using a small icing spatula, spread the white icing on top and partly down the sides of the loaves. Let cool completely before serving.

Makes 2 loaves

Onion-Herb Rolls

⅓ cup (3 fl oz/80 ml) olive oil

1¼ cups (6½ oz/200 g) finely chopped
yellow onion

2 cloves garlic, finely chopped

1 teaspoon minced fresh sage

1 teaspoon minced fresh rosemary

1 teaspoon minced fresh thyme

1 cup (8 fl oz/250 ml) warm water
(120°F/49°C)

1 tablespoon active dry yeast

3 tablespoons wheat bran

scant 1½ teaspoons salt

¼ teaspoon freshly ground pepper

about 3 cups (15 oz/470 g) all-purpose
(plain) flour

*Fragrant with sage, rosemary and thyme, these rolls are perfect with
Thanksgiving dinner.*

*I*n a heavy frying pan over medium heat, warm the olive oil.
Add the onion and garlic and sauté, stirring, until tender, about
8 minutes. Stir in the herbs and sauté until the flavors have
blended, about 2 minutes. Remove from the heat and let cool.

Pour the warm water into a large bowl. Sprinkle the yeast over
the top and let stand until dissolved, about 1 minute. Stir in the
bran, salt and pepper, then mix in the onion mixture. Using a
wooden spoon, gradually beat in about 2½ cups (12½ oz/390 g)
flour to make a semisoft dough.

Transfer the dough to a floured work surface and knead,
adding flour as needed to prevent sticking, until just smooth
and elastic, about 5 minutes. Grease a large, clean bowl with
olive oil. Gather the dough into a ball, place in the bowl and
turn to coat with the oil. Cover the bowl with a clean kitchen
towel. Place in a warm, draft-free area until the dough is
doubled in volume, about 1 hour.

Punch down the dough and transfer to a lightly floured work
surface. Knead until smooth, about 2 minutes. Divide the dough
into 12 equal portions and form each portion into a strip about
7 inches (18 cm) long and 2 inches (5 cm) wide. Beginning at a
narrow end, roll up each strip to form a roll. Oil a baking sheet
with olive oil and place the rolls, seam side down and well apart.
Cover with the kitchen towel and let rise in a warm, draft-free
area until doubled in volume, about 35 minutes.

Meanwhile, position a rack in the middle of an oven and preheat to 400°F (200°C). Bake until the rolls are golden brown and
sound hollow when thumped on the bottoms, 15–18 minutes.
Serve warm.

Makes 12 rolls

Blueberry-Crumb Coffee Cake

Any mother would love to be served this simple, delicate coffee cake on Mother's Day—or any other special day. It can also be baked in a pan 8 inches (20 cm) square.

FOR THE TOPPING:

¼ cup (2 oz/60 g) firmly packed light brown sugar

2 tablespoons all-purpose (plain) flour

½ teaspoon ground cinnamon

3 tablespoons unsalted butter

¼ cup (1 oz/30 g) finely chopped pecans

FOR THE CAKE:

1½ cups (7½ oz/235 g) all-purpose (plain) flour

2 teaspoons baking powder

½ teaspoon baking soda (bicarbonate of soda)

¼ teaspoon salt

¼ teaspoon ground nutmeg

¾ cup (6 oz/185 g) granulated sugar

2 eggs

1½ teaspoons grated lemon zest

2 tablespoons unsalted butter, melted

1 cup (8 fl oz/250 ml) sour cream

⅔ cup (3 oz/90 g) blueberries

*P*osition a rack in the middle of an oven and preheat to 350°F (180°C). Butter a springform pan 8 inches (20 cm) in diameter and 3 inches (7.5 cm) deep.

To make the topping, in a small bowl, combine the brown sugar, flour and cinnamon. Add the butter and, using your fingertips or a pastry blender, blend the ingredients together until the mixture resembles coarse meal. Using a fork, stir in the pecans. Set aside.

To make the cake, in a medium bowl, sift together the flour, baking powder, baking soda, salt and nutmeg. In a large bowl, whisk together the granulated sugar, eggs, lemon zest and butter until light and pale, about 1 minute. Using a wooden spoon, stir in the flour mixture in 2 batches alternately with the sour cream, beginning and ending with the sour cream. Fold in the blueberries. Spoon the batter into the prepared pan. Sprinkle the topping evenly over the surface.

Bake until a toothpick inserted into the center comes out clean, about 30 minutes. Transfer to a rack and let cool until warm, about 15 minutes, then transfer to a serving plate and remove the pan sides. Cut into wedges and serve warm.

Makes one 8-inch (20-cm) cake; serves 8

Buckwheat-Fennel Crisp Bread

¼ cup (2 fl oz/60 ml) warm water
   (120°F/49°C)
1 tablespoon active dry yeast
1 teaspoon sugar
¾ cup (6 fl oz/180 ml) milk
½ cup (4 oz/125 g) unsalted butter,
   melted and cooled
½ teaspoon salt
½ teaspoon baking soda (bicarbonate
   of soda)
½ cup (2½ oz/75 g) buckwheat flour
about 2½ cups (12½ oz/390 g)
   all-purpose (plain) flour
1 tablespoon fennel seeds

Crisp bread is a Christmas tradition in Scandinavia. There, a hob-nailed rolling pin is used to roll out the dough, but poking the dough repeatedly with fork tines works well, too. Serve the bread plain, or topped with smoked salmon or gravlax and watercress, if you like.

*P*osition a rack in the middle of an oven and preheat to 350°F (180°C). Butter 2 baking sheets.

Pour the warm water into a large bowl. Sprinkle the yeast over the top. Stir in the sugar and let stand until the mixture is bubbly, about 5 minutes. Add the milk, melted butter, salt and baking soda to the yeast mixture and stir until well mixed. Add the buckwheat flour and, using a wooden spoon, beat until smooth, about 2 minutes. Beat in about 2¼ cups (11½ oz/360 g) of the all-purpose flour to make a dough that is semisoft but no longer sticky.

Transfer the dough to a lightly floured work surface and knead, adding flour as needed to prevent sticking, until smooth, about 5 minutes. Divide the dough in half. Roll out each half into a 9-by-11-inch (23-by-28-cm) rectangle about ⅛ inch (3 mm) thick. Pierce each rectangle all over with fork tines.

Carefully transfer a dough rectangle to each baking sheet. Sprinkle half of the fennel seeds evenly over each rectangle and then gently press the seeds into the dough. Using a pastry wheel or sharp knife, cut each rectangle into 24 rectangular pieces.

Bake until the breads are crisp and golden brown, about 25 minutes. Transfer the baking sheets to racks and let cool completely. Break the rectangles apart into crackers. Store in an airtight container at room temperature for up to 1 week.

Makes 48 crackers

Apricot-Almond Chocolate Chunk Coffee Ring

about 4⅔ cups (23½ oz/735 g)
   all-purpose (plain) flour

⅓ cup (3 oz/90 g) sugar

1 tablespoon quick-rise active dry yeast

½ teaspoon salt

¾ cup (6 fl oz/180 ml) milk

½ cup (4 oz/125 g) unsalted butter

2 eggs

½ teaspoon almond extract (essence)

¾ cup (7½ oz/235 g) apricot preserves

½ cup (3 oz/90 g) minced dried apricots

3 oz (90 g) European bittersweet
   chocolate, chopped

1 cup (4 oz/125 g) sliced (flaked)
   almonds, toasted (*see glossary,*
   page 106)

white icing (*recipe on page 13*)

*I*n the bowl of a heavy-duty mixer fitted with the dough hook, combine 2 cups (10 oz/315 g) of the flour, the sugar, yeast and salt. In a small saucepan over low heat, stir together the milk and butter until the butter melts and the mixture is 130°F (54°C). Add the milk mixture to the flour mixture and beat on medium-high speed until well mixed. Beat in the eggs and the almond extract. Beat in about 2½ cups (12½ oz/390 g) more flour to make a dough that is semisoft and no longer sticky.

Transfer the dough to a lightly floured work surface and knead, adding flour as necessary to prevent sticking, until smooth and elastic, about 5 minutes. Cover with a clean kitchen towel and let rest for 10 minutes.

Grease a baking sheet with butter. Knead the dough briefly, then roll it out into a 16-by-20-inch (40-by-50-cm) rectangle. Spread evenly with the preserves, leaving a ½-inch (12-mm) border uncovered. Sprinkle evenly with the apricots, chocolate and half of the almonds. Starting at a long side, roll up jelly-roll style and pinch the seam to seal. Bring the ends together, forming a ring, and place seam side down on the prepared baking sheet. Press the ends together to seal. Using a sharp knife, cut gashes on the bias around the top of the ring about 1 inch (2.5 cm) apart, 2 inches (5 cm) deep and to within 1 inch (2.5 cm) of the inner rim of the ring. Gently pull open the gashes. Cover with the kitchen towel and let rise in a warm, draft-free area until doubled in volume, about 40 minutes.

Position a rack in the middle of an oven and preheat to 375°F (190°C). Bake until golden brown, about 50 minutes. Transfer to a serving plate and let cool slightly. Drizzle with the icing and sprinkle evenly with the remaining almonds. Serve warm.

Makes one 12-inch (30-cm) coffee cake; serves 10

Holiday Cutout Cookies

1 cup (8 oz/250 g) unsalted butter,
  at room temperature
¾ cup (6 oz/185 g) sugar
3 egg yolks
1 piece vanilla bean, about 2 inches
  (5 cm) long
2½ cups (12½ oz/390 g) all-purpose
  (plain) flour
1 teaspoon baking powder
½ teaspoon salt

These classic Christmas cookies can be decorated in a variety of ways. They can be sprinkled with colored sugar crystals before baking, or decorated with white icing (recipe on page 13) using a pastry bag fitted with a plain tip or a small plastic bag with a corner snipped off.

In a bowl, using an electric mixer set on medium speed, beat together the butter and sugar until light and fluffy, about 4 minutes. Beat in the egg yolks, one at a time, beating well after each addition. Cut the vanilla bean in half lengthwise and, using a small, sharp knife, scrape the seeds into the butter mixture. Mix well. In a sifter, combine the flour, baking powder and salt. Sift the flour mixture directly onto the butter mixture. Reduce the mixer speed to low and beat until well mixed.

Divide the dough into 4 equal portions. Shape each portion into a ball and then flatten the balls into disks. Wrap the disks in plastic wrap and refrigerate overnight. (The dough can be prepared up to 3 days ahead.) Let it soften slightly at room temperature before continuing.

Position a rack in the upper third of an oven and preheat to 350°F (180°C). Butter 2 large baking sheets. On a lightly floured work surface, roll out a dough disk ¼ inch (6 mm) thick. Using cookie cutters, cut out desired shapes. Transfer the cutouts to the prepared baking sheets. Gather up and reroll the scraps and cut out more cookies. Then repeat with the remaining dough disks.

Bake until the cookies are golden on the edges, about 8 minutes. Transfer the cookies to racks and let cool completely. Store in an airtight container at room temperature for up to 1 week.

Makes 4–5 dozen cookies

Honey Anise Springerle

2 eggs
⅔ cup (5 oz/155 g) sugar
⅓ cup (4 oz/125 g) honey
1 teaspoon vanilla extract (essence)
1 teaspoon aniseeds
½ teaspoon grated orange zest
½ teaspoon grated lemon zest
about 2¾ cups (14 oz/440 g) all-
   purpose (plain) flour
1 teaspoon baking powder
generous ¼ teaspoon salt

These old-fashioned cookies were made by Germanic tribes as part of the pagan celebration of Julfest. Unwilling to sacrifice their own live-stock to the gods as tradition demanded, the poor offered miniature animal cookies similar to these fanciful ones during the midwinter festival. To make them, you must use a springerle rolling pin (see equipment, page 7) to press the decorative shapes onto the dough.

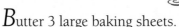

Butter 3 large baking sheets.

In a bowl, using an electric mixer set on high speed, beat the eggs until very pale and airy, about 3 minutes. Gradually add the sugar and continue beating until the mixture drops from the beaters in a ribbon, about 5 minutes. Gradually beat in the honey, vanilla, aniseeds, and orange and lemon zests. In a sifter, combine the 2¾ cups (14 oz/440 g) flour, baking powder and salt. Sift the mixture directly onto the egg mixture and, using a rubber spatula, stir gently to incorporate the flour.

Transfer the dough to a lightly floured work surface and knead briefly. Roll out the dough into a rectangle about ¼ inch (6 mm) thick. Lightly flour a springerle rolling pin, then firmly but gently roll it over the dough. Cut into cookies and transfer the cookies to the prepared baking sheets. Gather up and reroll the scraps and cut out more cookies. Cover the baking sheets with plastic wrap and let stand overnight at cool room temperature.

Position racks in the middle of an oven and preheat to 300°F (150°C). Bake until lightly golden and very crisp, about 20 minutes. Transfer to racks and let cool completely.

Store in an airtight container at room temperature for up to 2 weeks.

Makes about 6 dozen cookies

Lemon-Cardamom Tuiles

½ cup (4 oz/125 g) granulated sugar

¼ cup (1 oz/30 g) confectioners'
 (icing) sugar

1 tablespoon minced lemon zest

6 tablespoons (3 oz/90 g) unsalted
 butter, at room temperature

3 egg whites

2 teaspoons ground cardamom

½ teaspoon vanilla extract (essence)

¼ teaspoon salt

½ cup (2½ oz/75 g) all-purpose
 (plain) flour

These elegant, wafer-thin French cookies have a citrus and spice fragrance. Tuiles ("tiles") are thin cookies that are pressed around a rolling pin while still hot to produce a shape resembling a curved roof tile.

Position a rack in the middle of an oven and preheat to 350°F (180°C). Generously butter 2 nonstick baking sheets.

In a food processor fitted with the metal blade, combine the two sugars and lemon zest. Process until the lemon zest is very finely minced. Transfer to a large bowl and add the butter. Using an electric mixer set on medium speed, beat together the sugar mixture and butter until light and fluffy, about 3 minutes. Beat in the egg whites, cardamom, vanilla and salt until well mixed. Reduce the mixer speed to low and beat in the flour.

Drop 1 teaspoon of the batter onto a prepared baking sheet. Using the back of a spoon, spread the batter into a round about 3 inches (7.5 cm) in diameter. Repeat 5 more times, spacing the cookies evenly.

Bake until the cookies are golden brown on the edges, about 5 minutes. While the cookies are baking, form the next batch on the second baking sheet.

Remove from the oven and immediately run the tip of a small knife under the edge of a cookie. Carefully pick up the cookie and drape it over a long rolling pin. Quickly repeat with the remaining cookies; let cool completely on the pin.

Continue to bake and form the remaining batter in the same way, buttering the baking sheets before each new batch. Store in an airtight container at cool room temperature for up to 2 days.

Makes about 5 dozen cookies

Raspberry Linzer Heart Cookies

2 cups (8 oz/250 g) walnuts, toasted (*see glossary, page 106*) and cooled

2½ cups (12½ oz/390 g) all-purpose (plain) flour

1 cup (8 oz/250 g) unsalted butter, at room temperature

1 cup (4 oz/125 g) confectioners' (icing) sugar, plus extra for dusting

2 egg yolks

½ cup (2 oz/60 g) cornstarch (cornflour)

raspberry jam

*I*n a food processor fitted with the metal blade, process the walnuts and 1 cup (5 oz/155 g) of the flour until the nuts are finely ground; do not overprocess. Set aside.

In a bowl, using an electric mixer set on medium speed, beat together the butter and the 1 cup (4 oz/125 g) sugar until fluffy, about 4 minutes. Beat in the egg yolks, one at a time, beating well after each addition. Reduce the speed to low and beat in the walnut mixture, the remaining flour and the cornstarch until blended.

Divide the dough into 4 equal portions. Shape each portion into a ball and then flatten the balls into disks. Wrap the disks in plastic wrap and refrigerate overnight.

Position a rack in the upper third of an oven and preheat to 325°F (165°C). Butter 2 large baking sheets. On a lightly floured work surface, roll out a dough disk ¼ inch (6 mm) thick. Using a heart-shaped cookie cutter 2½ inches (6 cm) in diameter, cut out hearts. Transfer half of the hearts to a prepared baking sheet. Using a heart-shaped cookie cutter 1½ inches (4 cm) in diameter, cut out a heart from the center of each of the remaining heart cutouts, creating heart frames to use as cookie tops. Transfer to the other prepared sheet. Gather up and reroll the smaller hearts and scraps, then cut out more tops and bottoms. Repeat with the remaining disks.

Bake until just golden, about 15 minutes for bottoms and 12 minutes for tops. Let cool completely on racks.

Using a fine-mesh sieve, dust the heart frames evenly with confectioners' sugar. Using a small butter knife, spread raspberry jam over the tops of the large hearts. Place the sugar-dusted frames atop the larger hearts. Store in an airtight container at cool room temperature for up to 3 days.

Makes about 4 dozen cookies

Coconut-Almond Macaroons

3½ cups (14 oz/435 g) sweetened
   flaked coconut
1 cup (4 oz/125 g) sliced (flaked)
   almonds
½ cup (4 fl oz/125 ml) sweetened
   condensed milk
½ teaspoon almond extract (essence)
2 egg whites
1 tablespoon sugar
pinch of salt
warm melted bittersweet chocolate
   (*see glossary, page 104*)

As moist and chewy as candy bars, these cookies make a nice treat for Passover.

Position a rack in the middle of an oven and preheat to 350°F (180°C). Grease 2 large baking sheets with solid vegetable shortening.

In a baking pan, combine 1½ cups (6 oz/185 g) of the coconut and the almonds. Bake, stirring occasionally, until golden, about 12 minutes. Remove from the oven; let cool. Leave the oven set at 350°F (180°C).

In a large bowl, combine the cooled coconut mixture, the remaining 2 cups (8 oz/250 g) coconut, condensed milk and almond extract. In another large bowl, using an electric mixer set on high speed, beat together the egg whites, sugar and salt until soft peaks form. Using a rubber spatula, gently fold the egg whites into the coconut mixture.

Using a large spoon, form mounds 2 inches (5 cm) in diameter on the prepared sheets, spacing them 2 inches (5 cm) apart. Bake until the cookies are golden brown, about 10 minutes. Transfer to racks and let cool completely.

Line 2 baking sheets with waxed paper. Dip the bottoms of the cookies into the melted chocolate and transfer chocolate-side down to the prepared baking sheets. Refrigerate until the chocolate is set. Store the cookies in an airtight container at cool room temperature for up to 4 days.

Makes about 18 cookies

Pfeffernusse

2¼ cups (11½ oz/360 g) all-purpose
   (plain) flour
½ teaspoon salt
½ teaspoon ground black pepper
½ teaspoon crushed aniseeds
½ teaspoon ground cinnamon
¼ teaspoon baking soda (bicarbonate
   of soda)
¼ teaspoon ground allspice
¼ teaspoon ground nutmeg
⅛ teaspoon ground cloves
½ cup (4 oz/125 g) unsalted butter,
   at room temperature
¾ cup (6 oz/185 g) firmly packed
   light brown sugar
¼ cup (2 fl oz/60 ml) light (unsulfured)
   molasses
1 egg
about 2 cups (8 oz/250 g) confectioners'
   (icing) sugar for dusting

This German version of the traditional northern European "pepper nut" cookies are a family favorite at Christmastime.

*I*n a medium bowl, sift together the flour, salt, pepper, aniseeds, cinnamon, baking soda, allspice, nutmeg and cloves. In a large bowl, using an electric mixer set on medium speed, beat together the butter, brown sugar and molasses until light and fluffy, about 4 minutes. Beat in the egg. Reduce the mixer speed to low and beat in the flour mixture. Cover and refrigerate for several hours.

Position a rack in the middle of an oven and preheat to 350°F (180°C). Butter 2 baking sheets.

Scoop up pieces of the dough and roll between your palms into balls 1½ inches (4 cm) in diameter. Place the balls on the baking sheets, spacing them about 2 inches (5 cm) apart.

Bake until the cookies are golden brown on the bottom and firm to the touch, about 14 minutes. Transfer the baking sheets to racks and let the cookies cool slightly on the sheets. Place the confectioners' sugar in a sturdy paper bag. Drop a few cookies into the bag, close the top securely and shake gently to coat the warm cookies with the sugar. Transfer to racks and let cool completely. Repeat with the remaining cookies.

Store in an airtight container at cool room temperature for up to 1 week.

Makes about 2½ dozen cookies

Hazelnut Biscotti

1 cup (8 oz/250 g) unsalted butter,
  at room temperature
3 cups (1½ lb/750 g) sugar
4 eggs
6 cups (30 oz/940 g) all-purpose
  (plain) flour
2 teaspoons baking soda (bicarbonate
  of soda)
1 teaspoon salt
2 cups (10 oz/315 g) hazelnuts
  (filberts), toasted and skinned
  (*see glossary, page 106*)
warm melted bittersweet chocolate
  (*see glossary, page 104*), for dipping

The simplicity of these Italian cookies is appealing, but, if you like, you can add 1 tablespoon grated orange zest and 1 cup (4 oz/125 g) dried pitted sour cherries with the first addition of flour.

*P*osition racks in the middle of an oven and preheat to 325°F (165°C). Butter 2 large baking sheets.

In a large bowl, using an electric mixer set on medium speed, beat together the butter and sugar just until combined. Beat in the eggs. In another large bowl, stir together the flour, baking soda and salt. On low speed, beat half of the flour mixture into the butter mixture until combined. Beat in the hazelnuts and then the remaining flour mixture.

Transfer the dough to a lightly floured work surface and knead briefly until the dough holds together. Divide the dough into 4 equal mounds. Shape each mound into a loaf 9 inches (23 cm) long and 3 inches (7.5 cm) wide. Place the loaves on the prepared baking sheets.

Bake until the loaves are golden and firm when the tops are lightly pressed, about 1 hour. Remove from the oven and let cool slightly on the baking sheets. Leave the oven set at 325°F (165°C).

Using a spatula, carefully transfer the loaves to a work surface. Using a long, serrated knife, cut crosswise on a slight diagonal into slices ½ inch (12 mm) thick. Arrange the slices, cut side down, on the baking sheets. Return to the oven and bake the cookies until golden and crisp, about 45 minutes. Transfer to racks and let cool completely.

Dip one side of each cooled cookie into the melted chocolate and set chocolate-side up on baking sheets. Refrigerate until the chocolate is set. Store in an airtight container at room temperature for up to 1 week.

Makes about 5 dozen cookies

Pine Nut Bars

½ cup (4 oz/125 g) unsalted butter

⅔ cup (4 oz/125 g) pine nuts

1 piece vanilla bean, about 2 inches (5 cm) long, split in half lengthwise

½ teaspoon grated orange zest

1 cup (7 oz/220 g) firmly packed light brown sugar

2 eggs

½ teaspoon baking soda (bicarbonate of soda)

¼ teaspoon salt

1 cup (5 oz/155 g) all-purpose (plain) flour

FOR THE TOPPING:

6 tablespoons (3 fl oz/90 ml) heavy (double) cream

1 tablespoon unsalted butter

4½ oz (140 g) European white chocolate, chopped

24 pine nuts, optional

24 small orange zest curls, optional

These moist and sophisticated bar cookies are a good addition to a Christmas cookie platter.

*P*osition a rack in the middle of an oven and preheat to 350°F (180°C). Butter a 7-by-11-inch (18-by-28-cm) baking pan.

In a heavy saucepan over medium heat, melt the butter. Add the pine nuts, vanilla bean and orange zest and cook, stirring, until the pine nuts are golden brown, about 3 minutes. Remove from the heat.

Remove the vanilla bean from the saucepan and, using the tip of a sharp knife, scrape the seeds into the pan. Discard the pod. Stir in the brown sugar. Let cool slightly, then whisk in the eggs and stir in the baking soda, salt and then the flour.

Pour the batter into the prepared pan. Bake until a toothpick inserted into the center comes out clean, about 20 minutes. Transfer to a rack and let cool completely. Press down gently on the edges to flatten if necessary.

To make the topping, in a small, heavy saucepan, combine the cream and butter and bring to a boil. Remove from the heat and whisk in the white chocolate. Return the pan to low heat and stir until the chocolate melts and the mixture is smooth, about 30 seconds.

Pour the topping over the cooled uncut bars in the pan. Tilt the pan to spread the topping evenly. Refrigerate until the topping is almost set, about 8 minutes.

With a knife, score the topping into 24 equal bars. Garnish each rectangle with a pine nut and an orange zest curl, if desired. When the topping is set, cut along the marks into bars.

Store in an airtight container at cool room temperature for up to 3 days.

Makes 2 dozen cookies

Mexican Wedding Cakes

½ cup (4 oz/125 g) unsalted butter, at room temperature

⅓ cup (1½ oz/45 g) confectioners' (icing) sugar, plus about 2 cups (8 oz/250 g) for dusting (optional)

½ teaspoon vanilla extract (essence)

¼ teaspoon salt

1 cup (5 oz/155 g) all-purpose (plain) flour

2 tablespoons masa harina

¾ cup (3 oz/90 g) pecans, toasted (*see glossary, page 106*), cooled and chopped

warm melted bittersweet chocolate (*see glossary, page 104*), for dipping (optional)

multicolored sprinkles, for dipping (optional)

These cookies are served at Christmastime celebrations as well as at weddings. Masa harina, a flour made from treated corn and commonly used to make tortillas, can be found in Mexican markets and well-stocked food stores.

*P*osition a rack in the middle of an oven and preheat to 300°F (150°C). In a bowl, using an electric mixer on medium speed, beat together the butter and the ⅓ cup (1½ oz/45 g) confectioners' sugar until very light and fluffy, about 4 minutes. Beat in the vanilla and salt. Reduce the speed to low and beat in the flour and masa harina, then stir in the pecans.

Scoop up small pieces of the dough and roll them between your palms to form 1-inch (2.5-cm) balls or cylinders 2 inches (5 cm) long and ½ inch (12 mm) in diameter. Arrange the balls or cylinders 1 inch (2.5 cm) apart on an ungreased baking sheet. Bake until the cookies begin to turn golden, about 25 minutes. Transfer the baking sheet to a rack and let the cookies cool slightly on the sheet. Repeat with the remaining dough on another baking sheet.

If round cookies were made, place the confectioners' sugar in a sturdy paper bag for dredging. Drop a few warm round cookies into the bag, close the top securely and shake gently to coat the cookies with the sugar. Transfer to a rack and let cool completely.

If cylindrical cookies were made, dip one end of each cookie into the melted chocolate and then into sprinkles, if desired. Place on an aluminum foil–lined baking sheet and refrigerate until the chocolate is set.

Store sugar- or chocolate-coated cookies in an airtight container at cool room temperature for up to 3 days.

Makes about 2 dozen cookies

Hawaiian Shortbread Wedges

1 cup (4 oz/125 g) sweetened shredded
  coconut
¾ cup (4 oz/125 g) coarsely chopped
  macadamia nuts
½ cup (4 oz/125 g) unsalted butter,
  at room temperature
¾ cup (3 oz/90 g) confectioners'
  (icing) sugar
1 egg yolk
1 teaspoon vanilla extract (essence)
¼ teaspoon salt
1⅓ cups (7 oz/220 g) all-purpose
  (plain) flour
¼ cup (1½ oz/45 g) chopped dried
  mango

*Studded with macadamia nuts, dried mango and shredded coco-
nut, these delicious tropical treats are ideal for giving as gifts or
enjoying at the end of a luau feast.*

*P*osition a rack in the middle of an oven and preheat to
325°F (165°C).

On a baking sheet, mix together the coconut and macadamia nuts. Bake, stirring occasionally, until lightly toasted,
about 8 minutes. Remove from the oven and let cool. Leave
the oven set at 325°F (165°C).

In a bowl, using an electric mixer set on medium speed,
beat the butter until fluffy, about 4 minutes. Add the sugar
and beat, stopping once or twice to scrape the sugar to the
center of the bowl with a rubber spatula, until light, about
1 minute. Beat in the egg yolk, vanilla and salt. On low
speed, beat in the flour and then the coconut mixture and
the mango to form a soft dough.

Divide the dough in half and press each half into a round
cake pan 9 inches (23 cm) in diameter. Using fork tines,
mark each round into 8 wedges.

Bake until the shortbread is golden brown, about 20
minutes. Transfer the pans to a rack and, using the marks
as guides, cut into wedges. Let cool completely. Store in
an airtight container at room temperature for up to 3 days.

Makes 16 cookies

Sesame-Almond Ginger Lace Cookies

½ cup (2 oz/60 g) sliced (flaked)
  almonds
½ cup (2½ oz/75 g) all-purpose
  (plain) flour
1 cup (7 oz/220 g) firmly packed
  golden brown sugar
⅓ cup (1 oz/30 g) sesame seeds
⅓ cup (1 oz/30 g) rolled oats
3 tablespoons minced crystallized
  ginger
2 teaspoons grated orange zest
½ teaspoon baking powder
¼ teaspoon salt
½ cup (4 oz/125 g) unsalted butter,
  melted and cooled
¼ cup (2 fl oz/60 ml) milk

These Asian-inspired cookies are wonderful accompaniments to fruit sorbets, or serve them with fresh lychee nuts for a truly exotic dessert. They are also delicious dipped in melted bitter-sweet chocolate, or you can make 4 dozen small cookies, spread half of them with melted chocolate and then top with the remaining cookies to form cookie sandwiches.

Position a rack in the upper third of an oven and preheat to 350°F (180°C).

In a bowl, combine the almonds, flour, brown sugar, sesame seeds, oats, crystallized ginger, orange zest, baking powder and salt. Using a spoon, stir in the melted butter and milk. Let stand for 10 minutes.

Line a baking sheet with aluminum foil. To form the cookies, working in batches, drop the batter by level tablespoonfuls onto the foil, spacing them about 3 inches (7.5 cm) apart. Bake until the cookies are bubbly and browned on the edges, about 12 minutes.

Carefully remove the foil from the baking sheet and let the cookies cool on a flat surface. While the cookies are cooling, line the baking sheet with another sheet of aluminum foil and form and bake the remaining batter in the same way.

Using a small spatula to lift the edges, remove the cookies from the foil. Store in an airtight container at room temperature for up to 3 days.

Makes about 2 dozen cookies

Gingerbread Cookies

¾ cup (6 oz/185 g) unsalted butter,
   at room temperature
¾ cup (6 oz/185 g) firmly packed light
   brown sugar
¼ cup (2 fl oz/60 ml) light (unsulfured)
   molasses
2 egg yolks
2⅓ cups (12 oz/375 g) unbleached
   all-purpose (plain) flour
2 teaspoons ground cinnamon
2 teaspoons ground ginger
1 teaspoon ground allspice
½ teaspoon baking soda (bicarbonate
   of soda)
¼ teaspoon ground cloves
¼ teaspoon salt
white icing (*recipe on page 13*)

Pipe decorations onto these cookies using a pastry (piping) bag fitted with a plain tip or a small plastic bag with a corner snipped off. Or spread each cookie with a thin layer of the icing, let dry and then, using a tiny brush and food coloring, paint on decorations.

*I*n a bowl, using an electric mixer set on medium speed, beat together the butter, brown sugar and molasses until fluffy, about 3 minutes. Beat in the egg yolks. In a sifter, combine the flour, cinnamon, ginger, allspice, baking soda, cloves and salt. Sift the flour mixture directly onto the butter mixture. Reduce the mixer speed to low and beat until well combined. Gather the dough into a ball; it will be soft. Wrap in plastic wrap and refrigerate overnight.

Position racks in the upper third of the oven and preheat to 375°F (190°C). Butter 2 large, heavy baking sheets.

Remove one-third of the dough from the refrigerator. On a lightly floured work surface, roll it out ¼ inch (6 mm) thick. Using a figure-shaped cookie cutter 5 inches (13 cm) long, cut out gingerbread people. Carefully transfer the cookies to the prepared baking sheet, placing them about 1 inch (2.5 cm) apart. Gather up the scraps into a ball, wrap in plastic wrap and chill. Repeat rolling and cutting out the cookies with the remaining dough, in 2 batches. Then reroll the scraps and cut out more cookies.

Bake until the cookies begin to turn golden brown on the edges, about 10 minutes. Transfer to racks and let cool.

Decorate the cooled cookies with the white icing as desired (see note). Store in an airtight container at room temperature for up to 1 week.

Makes about 20 cookies

Sour Cream–Pumpkin Pie

½ recipe (1 disk) pie or tart pastry
   (recipe on page 11)
1 can (1 lb/500 g) pumpkin purée
1 cup (8 fl oz/250 ml) sour cream
⅔ cup (5 oz/155 g) sugar
3 eggs
1 tablespoon all-purpose (plain) flour
1 teaspoon ground cinnamon
½ teaspoon ground nutmeg
½ teaspoon ground ginger

FOR THE TOPPING:
1 cup (8 fl oz/250 ml) heavy (double)
   cream, chilled
2 tablespoons sugar
½ cup (4 fl oz/125 ml) sour cream

The addition of sour cream gives a wonderful light and creamy texture to this old Thanksgiving favorite.

On a lightly floured work surface, roll out the pastry into a round about 13 inches (33 cm) in diameter and ⅛ inch (3 mm) thick. Drape the pastry round over the rolling pin and carefully transfer it to a 9-inch (23-cm) pie pan. Press the pastry firmly but gently into the pan. Trim the edge so that there is about a 1-inch (2.5-cm) overhang. Fold under the overhang and flute the edges. Freeze the pastry shell until firm, about 20 minutes.

Position a rack in the bottom third of an oven and preheat to 400°F (200°C).

Line the pastry shell with parchment paper or aluminum foil and fill with dried beans or pie weights. Bake until the pastry shell is set, about 15 minutes. Remove the beans or weights and the paper or foil. Continue baking the pastry shell until golden brown, about 20 minutes longer. Transfer to a rack and let cool completely. Reduce the oven temperature to 325°F (165°C).

In a large bowl, combine the pumpkin, sour cream, sugar, eggs, flour, cinnamon, nutmeg and ginger. Whisk until smooth.

Pour the pumpkin mixture into the cooled pastry shell. Bake until the filling is just set, about 45 minutes; check the pie periodically and cover the edges with aluminum foil if the crust browns too quickly. Transfer to a rack and let cool completely.

To make the topping, in a chilled bowl, using an electric mixer set on high speed, beat together the cream and sugar until stiff peaks form. Using a rubber spatula, fold the sour cream into the whipped cream.

Cut the pie into wedges. Place each wedge on a serving plate and spoon on the topping.

Makes one 9-inch (23-cm) pie; serves 8

Apple-Cinnamon Pie

1 recipe (2 disks) pie or tart pastry
(recipe on page 11)

7 or 8 large tart green apples, such as
Granny Smith, halved, cored and
thinly sliced

⅔ cup (5 oz/155 g) plus 1 tablespoon
sugar

2 tablespoons quick-cooking granulated
tapioca

1 tablespoon ground cinnamon, plus
extra for topping

½ teaspoon freshly grated nutmeg

*Here is an old-fashioned American pie that will shine on your
Thanksgiving or Fourth of July table.*

Position a rack in the bottom third of an oven and preheat to
400°F (200°C). On a lightly floured work surface, roll out 1
pastry disk into a round about 13 inches (33 cm) in diameter
and ⅛ inch (3 mm) thick. Drape the pastry round over the
rolling pin and carefully transfer it to a 9-inch (23-cm) pie pan.
Press the pastry firmly but gently into the pan.

In a large bowl, combine the apples, the ⅔ cup (5 oz/155 g)
sugar, the tapioca, 1 tablespoon cinnamon and the nutmeg.
Toss gently until all ingredients are evenly distributed. Spoon
the filling into the crust.

On the lightly floured surface, roll out the remaining pastry
disk into a second round about 12 inches (30 cm) in diameter.
Drape the pastry round over the rolling pin and transfer it to
the pie, positioning it over the filling. Trim the edges of the
pastry rounds so there is about a 1-inch (2.5-cm) overhang.
Press firmly around the rim of the pan to seal the crusts
together, then fold under the overhang and flute the edges.
Using a small, sharp knife, cut 4 equidistant vents around the
center of the top crust for the steam to escape. Gather up and
reroll the scraps, then cut into decorative shapes. Moisten the
bottoms lightly with water and place the cutouts on the pie top.

Sprinkle the top crust with the remaining 1 tablespoon sugar
and a little cinnamon. Bake until golden brown and the juices
are bubbling, about 1 hour; check the pie periodically and cover
the edges with aluminum foil if they brown too quickly.

Transfer to a rack and let cool slightly. Serve warm or at room
temperature.

Makes one 9-inch (23-cm) double-crust pie; serves 8

Miniature Truffle Tartlets

FOR THE PASTRY:

1 cup (5 oz/155 g) unbleached all-
   purpose (plain) flour

¼ cup (2 oz/60 g) sugar

3 tablespoons unsweetened cocoa

¼ teaspoon salt

6 tablespoons (3 oz/90 g) chilled
   unsalted butter, cut into pieces

1 egg yolk

bittersweet chocolate ganache, warm
   (recipe on page 12)

fresh raspberries or toasted and
   skinned hazelnuts (filberts)
   (see glossary, page 106)

Make these small, delicate sweets for putting out on your annual New Year's or Christmas Eve buffet table. Sugared violets, orange peel or rose petals would also make good garnishes. The tart pans can be lined with the pastry up to 1 week in advance, wrapped in plastic wrap and frozen.

*T*o make the pastry, in a bowl, combine the flour, sugar, cocoa and salt. Add the butter and, using your fingertips or a pastry blender, blend the ingredients together until the mixture resembles coarse meal. Using a fork, stir in the egg yolk until fully combined. The dough should be soft but not wet.

   Spray about twenty-two 2–3-inch (5–7.5-cm) tartlet pans or 22 muffin pan cups with nonstick vegetable oil cooking spray. Pinch off tablespoon-sized portions of the dough and, using your fingertips, press the dough evenly onto the bottom and up the sides of each pan or cup. Freeze until firm, about 15 minutes.

   Preheat an oven to 400°F (200°C).

   Place the tartlet pans on baking sheets and bake until the crusts just begin to brown on the edges, about 20 minutes. Transfer the baking sheets holding the tartlet pans to racks and let cool completely.

   With the top of a sharp knife, carefully loosen the crusts, then lift the crusts out of the pans and place on the baking sheets. Pour the ganache into the crusts, dividing it evenly. Chill until the ganache is almost set, about 4 minutes.

   Top each tartlet with a raspberry or hazelnut. Cover and chill until firm, about 1 hour.

   Serve immediately, or wrap in plastic wrap and store in the refrigerator for up to 1 day.

Makes twenty-two 2–3-inch (5–7.5-cm) tartlets

Summer Berry Pie

1½ cups (6 oz/185 g) sugar

¼ cup (1 oz/30 g) cornstarch
(cornflour)

3 tablespoons fresh lemon juice

4½ cups (18 oz/560 g) raspberries

4½ cups (18 oz/560 g) blackberries
or boysenberries

1 recipe (2 disks) pie or tart pastry
(recipe on page 11)

A celebration of flavors, this colorful pie is perfect for a barbecue to celebrate Independence Day. Serve with vanilla ice cream.

*I*n a large, heavy saucepan, stir together the sugar, cornstarch and lemon juice. Add the berries and toss gently with the sugar mixture. Place over medium heat and bring to a boil, stirring very gently. Boil, stirring, until the mixture becomes thick and clear, about 6 minutes. Transfer to a bowl and let cool.

Position a rack in the bottom third of an oven and preheat to 400°F (200°C).

On a lightly floured work surface, roll out 1 pastry disk into a round about 14 inches (35 cm) in diameter and ⅛ inch (3 mm) thick. Drape the pastry round over the rolling pin and carefully transfer it to a 9-inch (23-cm) deep-dish pie pan with 2-inch (5-cm) sides. Press the pastry firmly but gently into the pan.

Roll out the remaining pastry disk into a round about 13 inches (33 cm) in diameter and ⅛ inch (3 mm) thick. Using a sharp knife, cut vents decoratively into the pastry round.

Pour the cooled filling into the pastry-lined pan. Drape the pastry round over the rolling pin and carefully transfer it to the pie, positioning it over the filling. Trim the edges of the pastry rounds so that there is about a 1-inch (2.5-cm) overhang. Press firmly around the rim of the pan to seal the crusts together, then fold under the overhang and flute the edges.

Bake until the crust is golden and the juices are bubbling, about 45 minutes; check the pie periodically and cover the edges with aluminum foil if they brown too quickly. Transfer to a rack and let cool completely before serving.

Makes one 9-inch (23-cm) double-crust deep-dish pie; serves 8

Twelfth Night Jam Tart

1 recipe (2 disks) pie or tart pastry
(recipe on page 11)

1 egg

2 tablespoons heavy (double) cream

about ¼ cup (2½ oz/75 g) each of
5 assorted jams, such as apricot,
raspberry, blueberry, plum, cherry,
marmalade or blackberry, in any
combination

For centuries, star-shaped tarts like this one have been served at the celebration of Twelfth Night, which marks the twelfth day after Christmas. This tart is good served warm with vanilla ice cream.

*P*osition a rack in the middle of an oven and preheat to 400°F (200°C).

On a lightly floured work surface, roll out 1 pastry disk into a round about 11 inches (28 cm) in diameter and ⅛ inch (3 mm) thick. Drape the pastry round over the rolling pin and transfer it to a heavy baking sheet. Using a small, sharp knife, and starting about 1½ inches (4 cm) in from the edge, mark the points of a clock face on the pastry round. Using the knife, draw a line (without cutting all the way through) from 12 o'clock to 4 o'clock, from 4 to 8 o'clock, and from 8 to 12 o'clock. Then draw a line from 6 to 2 o'clock, from 2 to 10 o'clock and from 10 to 6 o'clock, to form a 6-point star.

On the floured surface, roll out the remaining dough disk into a round 11 inches (28 cm) in diameter and about ⅛ inch (3 mm) thick. Using the knife, cut the round into strips ½ inch (12 mm) wide. Lay a dough strip on each of the lines you just cut onto the pastry round, to form the 6-point star. Cut off the edges of the strips evenly with the outline of the clock face. Fold the uncovered edge of the bottom crust inward so that the edge is even with the points of the star and forms a rim.

In a small bowl, whisk together the egg and cream until well blended. Brush the egg mixture over the surface of the tart. Bake until golden brown, about 20 minutes. Remove from the oven and fill the indentations with the assorted jams. Return to the oven and bake until the jams are set, about 5 minutes.

Transfer to a rack. Serve warm or at room temperature.

Makes one 9-inch (23-cm) tart; serves 8

Orange-Spice Nut Tartlets

½ recipe (1 disk) pie or tart pastry
   (recipe on page 11)
¾ cup (6 fl oz/180 ml) heavy (double)
   cream
⅓ cup (3 oz/90 g) granulated sugar
3 tablespoons firmly packed light
   brown sugar
3 tablespoons honey
1 tablespoon unsweetened cocoa
⅓ cup (1½ oz/45 g) chopped walnuts,
   lightly toasted (see glossary, page 106)
⅓ cup (1½ oz/45 g) sliced (flaked)
   almonds, lightly toasted (see glossary,
   page 106)
⅓ cup (2 oz/60 g) hazelnuts (filberts),
   toasted and skinned (see glossary,
   page 106), then cooled and chopped
⅓ cup (2 oz/60 g) diced dried
   Calimyrna figs
2 teaspoons grated orange zest
½ teaspoon ground cinnamon
½ teaspoon ground nutmeg
½ teaspoon ground coriander
pinch of ground cloves
whipped cream, optional

The flavors in this sophisticated dessert are reminiscent of the Italian dried-fruit-and-nut Christmas confection called panforte.

On a lightly floured work surface, roll out the dough into a round about 14 inches (35 cm) in diameter and ⅛ inch (3 mm) thick. Cut the round into quarters. Ease each quarter into a tartlet pan with a removable bottom 4½ inches (11 cm) in diameter and ¾ inch (2 cm) deep. Trim the edges even with the rim and patch any holes with the scraps. Place on a baking sheet and freeze until firm, about 20 minutes.

Position a rack in the middle of an oven and preheat to 400°F (200°C).

Line the pastry shells with parchment paper or aluminum foil and fill with dried beans or pie weights. Bake until the crusts are set, about 15 minutes. Remove the beans or weights and the paper or foil. Transfer the baking sheet holding the shells to a rack and let cool. Leave the oven set at 400°F (200°C).

In a saucepan, combine the cream, granulated sugar, brown sugar, honey and cocoa. Bring to a boil over high heat, stirring to dissolve the sugars. Boil, stirring occasionally, until very thick, about 4 minutes. Remove from the heat and let cool slightly. Stir in all the nuts, the figs, orange zest, cinnamon, nutmeg, coriander and cloves.

Divide the filling evenly among the pastry shells. Bake until the filling is bubbling and is darker around the edges, about 25 minutes. Transfer the sheet to a rack and let cool to warm.

Run a small, sharp knife around the edges of the pans to loosen the crusts, then remove the pan sides. Let cool completely.

Serve with whipped cream, if desired.

Makes four 4½-inch (11-cm) tartlets; serves 4

Pecan-Cranberry Pie

½ recipe (1 disk) pie or tart pastry
  (recipe on page 11)
3 eggs
¾ cup (6 oz/185 g) firmly packed
  golden brown sugar
½ cup (4 fl oz/125 ml) light corn syrup
¼ cup (2 oz/60 g) unsalted butter,
  melted and cooled
2 tablespoons light (unsulfured)
  molasses
1 teaspoon vanilla extract (essence)
1½ cups (6 oz/185 g) pecans, toasted
  (see glossary, page 106), cooled and
  coarsely chopped
1½ cups (6 oz/185 g) cranberries

Cranberries add a wonderful tartness to this sweet, rich southern pie. It's a delicious addition to a Thanksgiving or Christmas menu or to follow the traditional Southern black-eyed peas on New Year's Day.

On a lightly floured work surface, roll out the pastry about 13 inches (33 cm) in diameter and ⅛ inch (3 mm) thick. Drape the pastry round over the rolling pin and carefully transfer it to a 9-inch (23-cm) pie pan. Press the pastry firmly but gently into the pan. Trim the edge so that there is about a 1-inch (2.5-cm) overhang. Fold under the overhang. Flute the edges or gather up and reroll the scraps, cut into decorative shapes, then moisten the bottoms lightly with water and place the cutouts along the pie rim. Freeze until firm, about 20 minutes.

Position a rack in the bottom third of an oven and preheat to 400°F (200°C).

In a large bowl, combine the eggs, brown sugar, corn syrup, melted butter, molasses and vanilla. Whisk until smooth. Stir in the pecans and cranberries.

Pour the pecan-cranberry filling into the pastry shell. Bake until the center of the filling is set, about 45 minutes; check the pie periodically and cover the edges with aluminum foil if the crust browns too quickly.

Transfer to a rack and let cool completely before serving.

Makes one 9-inch (23-cm) pie; serves 8–12

Eggnog Tart

½ recipe (1 disk) pie or tart pastry
   (recipe on page 11)
1 cup (8 fl oz/250 ml) heavy (double)
   cream
¼ cup (2 fl oz/60 ml) milk
1 piece vanilla bean, 3 inches (7.5 cm)
   long, split in half lengthwise
5 egg yolks
¼ cup (2 oz/60 g) sugar
1 tablespoon brandy
freshly grated nutmeg

Accompany wedges of this Christmastime tart with a fruit compote.

On a lightly floured work surface, roll out the pastry dough into a round about 12 inches (30 cm) in diameter and ⅛ inch (3 mm) thick. Drape the pastry round over the rolling pin and ease it into a 9-inch (23-cm) tart pan with a removable bottom. Trim the edges even with the rim. Freeze the shell until firm, about 20 minutes.

Position a rack in the middle of an oven and preheat to 400°F (200°C). Line the pastry shell with parchment paper or aluminum foil and fill with dried beans or pie weights. Bake until the pastry shell is set, about 15 minutes. Remove the beans or weights and the paper or foil. Continue baking until golden brown, about 20 minutes longer. Transfer to a rack and let cool completely. Reduce the oven temperature to 325°F (165°C).

In a heavy, medium saucepan over medium heat, combine the cream, milk and vanilla bean and bring to a simmer. Remove from the heat. Cover and let stand for 10 minutes. In a large bowl, whisk together the egg yolks and sugar until blended. Return the cream mixture to medium-high heat and bring to a boil. Remove from the heat. Gradually add the cream mixture to the egg yolk mixture, whisking constantly. Place over low heat and cook, stirring constantly, until the mixture thickens and coats the back of a spoon, about 4 minutes; do not allow it to boil. Remove from the heat and whisk in the brandy. Remove the vanilla bean and discard. Let cool slightly.

Pour the custard into the cooled pastry shell and sprinkle nutmeg lightly over the top. Bake until just set, about 20 minutes. Let cool completely on a rack before serving.

Makes one 9-inch (23-cm) tart; serves 8

Sweetheart Raspberry Tart

½ recipe (1 disk) pie or tart pastry (*recipe on page 11*)

2 oz (60 g) European bittersweet chocolate

vanilla pastry cream, hot (*recipe on page 12*)

¼ teaspoon unflavored gelatin

1 tablespoon framboise eau-de-vie

⅓ cup (3 fl oz/80 ml) heavy (double) cream, chilled

3 cups (¾ lb/375 g) fresh raspberries

Serve this tart to someone special on Valentine's Day. Framboise, a clear raspberry brandy, can be found in selected liquor stores.

On a lightly floured work surface, roll out the pastry dough into a round about 12 inches (30 cm) in diameter and ⅛ inch (3 mm) thick. Drape the pastry round over the rolling pin and ease it into a 9-inch (23-cm) tart pan with a removable bottom. Trim the edges even with the rim. Freeze the pastry shell until firm, about 20 minutes.

Position a rack in the middle of an oven and preheat to 400°F (200°C). Line the pastry shell with parchment paper or aluminum foil and fill with dried beans or pie weights. Bake until the pastry shell is set, about 15 minutes. Remove the beans or weights and the paper or foil. Continue baking until golden brown, about 20 minutes longer. Transfer to a rack and let cool completely.

In the top pan of a double boiler or a heatproof bowl placed over (not touching) simmering water, melt the chocolate, stirring until smooth. Using the back of a spoon, coat the inside bottom and sides of the pastry shell with the chocolate. Refrigerate until set, about 20 minutes. Meanwhile, make the pastry cream.

In a small bowl, dissolve the gelatin in the framboise and let stand for 10 minutes. Stir the gelatin mixture into the hot pastry cream. Let stand at room temperature, stirring occasionally, until cool but not set.

In a chilled bowl, using an electric mixer set on medium-high speed, whip the cream to form stiff peaks. Using a rubber spatula, fold the whipped cream into the pastry cream. Spread in the chocolate-lined shell. Refrigerate until set, about 1 hour.

Arrange the raspberries attractively over the pastry cream filling and serve within 4 hours.

Makes one 9-inch (23-cm) tart; serves 6

Pear and Mince Pie

1 recipe (2 disks) pie or tart pastry
  (recipe on page 11)

5 large pears, preferably Bosc, Comice
  or Anjou, peeled, halved, cored and
  chopped

1¼ cups (10 oz/315 g) prepared
  mincemeat

¼ cup (2 oz/60 g) firmly packed dark
  brown sugar

1 tablespoon all-purpose (plain) flour

1 teaspoon ground cinnamon

1 teaspoon grated orange zest

½ teaspoon ground allspice

⅛ teaspoon ground cloves

1 egg

1 tablespoon milk

Delicious for Christmas or Thanksgiving dinner, this dessert is a light version of the traditional wintertime mince pie. You can also top the pie with a solid crust rather than a lattice crust.

*P*osition a rack in the bottom third of an oven and preheat to 400°F (200°C). On a lightly floured work surface, roll out 1 pastry disk into a round about 11 inches (28 cm) in diameter and ⅛ inch (3 mm) thick. Drape the pastry round over the rolling pin and carefully transfer it to a 9-inch (23-cm) pie pan. Press the pastry firmly but gently into the pan and trim the edges flush with the pan rim.

In a large bowl, combine the pears, mincemeat, brown sugar, flour, cinnamon, orange zest, allspice and cloves. Using a large spoon, stir to mix well and set aside.

On the lightly floured surface, roll out the remaining pastry disk into a second round about ⅛ inch (3 mm) thick. Using a pastry cutter or a knife, cut out strips about ½ inch (12 mm) wide. Following the detailed instructions on page 11, use the pastry strips to make a lattice top on a lightly floured sheet of waxed paper, spoon the filling into the crust; secure the lattice on top as directed on page 11.

In a small bowl, whisk together the egg and milk until blended. Brush the egg mixture evenly over the crust. Bake until the crust is golden brown and the juices are bubbling, about 1 hour; check the pie periodically and cover the edges with aluminum foil if they brown too quickly.

Transfer to a rack and let cool briefly. Serve warm or at room temperature.

Make one 9-inch (23-cm) lattice-top pie; serves 8

Glossary

The following glossary defines terms specifically as they relate to holiday baking, including major and unusual ingredients and basic cooking techniques.

ALLSPICE
Sweet spice of Caribbean origin with a flavor suggesting a blend of **cinnamon, cloves** and **nutmeg,** hence its name. May be purchased as whole dried berries or ground.

ANISEEDS
Sweet licorice-flavored spice of Mediterranean origin, the small crescent-shaped seeds of a plant related to parsley. Generally sold as whole seeds, which may be crushed with a mortar and pestle.

BAKING POWDER
Commercial baking product combining three ingredients: **baking soda,** the source of the carbon-dioxide gas that causes quick batters and doughs to rise; an acid, such as cream of tartar, calcium acid phosphate or sodium aluminum sulphate, which, when the powder is combined with a liquid, causes the baking soda to release its gas; and a starch such as **cornstarch** (cornflour), to keep the powder from absorbing moisture.

BAKING SODA
Also known as bicarbonate of soda or sodium bicarbonate, the active component of **baking powder** and the source of the carbon dioxide gas that leavens batters and doughs. Often used on its own when acidic ingredients such as buttermilk, yogurt or citrus juices are present.

BRAN
The papery brown coating of a whole grain, usually removed during milling. Unless the type of grain is specified, the term usually refers to wheat bran.

BRANDY
Applies to any spirit distilled from fermented fruit juice. While the term most specifically refers to dry grape brandy, it also covers dry-to-sweet distillates of such fruits as apples and berries.

BUTTERMILK
Form of cultured low-fat or nonfat milk that contributes a tangy flavor and thick, creamy texture to quick batters and doughs. Its acidity also provides a boost to leavening agents such as **baking soda,** adding extra lightness.

CARDAMOM
Sweet, exotic-tasting spice (below) mainly used in Middle Eastern and Indian cooking and in European baking. Its small, round seeds, which grow enclosed inside a husklike pod, are best purchased whole, then ground with a spice grinder or with a mortar and pestle as needed.

CINNAMON
Popular sweet spice for flavoring baked goods. The aromatic bark of a type of evergreen tree, it is sold as whole dried strips—cinnamon sticks—or ground.

CLOVES
Rich and aromatic East African spice used whole or in its ground form to flavor both sweet and savory recipes.

CHOCOLATE & COCOA
For holiday baking, purchase the best-quality chocolate you can find, selecting the type specified in the recipe. Many cooks prefer the quality of European chocolate made in Switzerland, Belgium, France or Italy.

Bittersweet Chocolate
Lightly sweetened eating or baking chocolate that generally contains about 40 percent cocoa butter. Look for bittersweet chocolate that contains at least 50 percent cocoa butter.

White Chocolate
A chocolatelike product for eating or baking, made by combining pure cocoa butter with sugar, powdered milk and sometimes **vanilla.** Check labels to make sure that the white chocolate you buy is made exclusively with cocoa butter, without the addition of coconut oil or vegetable shortening.

Unsweetened Cocoa
Richly flavored, fine-textured powder ground from the solids left after much of the cocoa butter has been extracted from chocolate liquor. Cocoa powder specially treated to reduce its natural acidity, resulting in a darker color and more mellow flavor, is known as Dutch-process cocoa.

Chocolate Cookie Crumbs
Several commercial varieties of crisp, chocolate-flavored cookies are sold in food stores and may be crushed for using in pie and cheesecake crusts.

To Chop Chocolate
While a food processor fitted with the metal blade can be used, a sharp, heavy knife offers better control.

First, break the chocolate by hand into small chunks, handling it as little as possible to avoid melting. Then, using a heavy knife and a clean, dry, odor-free chopping surface, carefully chop into smaller pieces.

Steadying the knife blade with your hand, continue chopping across the pieces until the desired consistency is reached.

To Melt Chocolate
Put pieces of chocolate in the top pan of a double boiler over barely simmering water. Take care that the pan does not touch the water and that the water does not create steam. Stir gently until the chocolate melts.

Alternatively, create your own double boiler by setting a heat-proof bowl on the rim of a pan that holds simmering water.

To Make Chocolate Curls
Curls of chocolate make an attractive decoration for baked goods. To make curls, set a large block of imported chocolate in a warm place until slightly softened. Then, firmly drag the sharp edge of a large knife across the surface of the block to form long, thin curls.

COCONUT

For baking purposes, shredded or flaked coconut is sold ready-to-use in cans or plastic packages. The label indicates whether the product is sweetened or unsweetened; most baking recipes call for sweetened coconut. Be sure to purchase coconut products from a store with a rapid turnover, to ensure freshness.

CONDENSED MILK, SWEETENED

A canned product made by evaporating 60 percent of the water from whole milk, then sweetening it with sugar, for use as an ingredient in baked recipes and dessert sauces.

CORIANDER

Small, spicy-sweet seeds of the coriander plant, which is also called cilantro or Chinese parsley. Used whole or ground as a seasoning.

CORN SYRUP

Neutral-tasting syrup extracted from corn. Sold either as light corn syrup or dark corn syrup, which has added color and flavor.

CORNSTARCH

Fine, powdery flour ground from the endosperm of corn—the white heart of the kernel—and, because it contains no gluten, used to give a delicate texture to baked goods. Also known as cornflour.

CREAM, DEVONSHIRE

Also known as clotted cream. Originally from Devon, England, it has a thick, buttery texture and is often used as a topping for desserts.

CREAM, HEAVY

Whipping cream with a butterfat content of at least 36 percent. For the best flavor and cooking properties, purchase 100 percent natural fresh cream with a short shelf life printed on the carton; avoid long-lasting varieties that have been processed by ultraheat methods. In Britain, use double cream.

CREAM, SOUR

Commercial dairy product made from pasteurized sweet cream. Like **buttermilk**, its extra acidity boosts the leavening action of **baking soda**.

CREAM CHEESE

Smooth, white, mild-tasting cheese made from cream and milk, used on its own as a spread or as an ingredient that adds rich flavor and texture to baked goods. Some recipes call for cream cheese that has been softened to facilitate its blending with other ingredients. To soften cream cheese quickly, place it unwrapped on a microwaveproof plate or in a bowl, or wrap in waxed paper or plastic wrap, and put it in a microwave oven; with the oven set on high, heat the cream cheese for 20 seconds, stopping to check its consistency and repeating as necessary until soft enough to mash easily with a fork. Alternatively, if the cheese is enclosed in an airtight commercial wrapper, leave the cheese in its wrapper; immerse it in a bowl of hot water until the desired consistency is reached, 2–3 minutes.

DRIED & CANDIED FRUIT

Intensely flavored and satisfyingly chewy, many forms of sun-dried or kiln-dried fresh or candied fruits may be added to enhance baked goods. Select more recently dried and packaged fruits, which have a softer texture than older dried fruits. Dried fruits are usually found in specialty-food shops or baking sections of most food stores. Some of the most popular options, used in this book, include:

Apricots
Pitted whole or halved fruits, sweet and slightly tangy.

Blueberries
Kiln-dried whole blueberries, resembling raisins in shape and texture, with a deep blue-black color and an intense blueberry flavor.

Candied Citron and Orange Peel
Two of the most popular forms of candied fruit for baking, these are made by saturating pieces of orange or citron peel with a sugar syrup, then drying them.

Cherries
Ripe, sour red cherries that have been pitted and dried—usually in a kiln, with a little sugar added to help preserve them—to a consistency and shape resembling that of raisins.

Cranberries
Kiln-dried, lightly sugared tart red berries that resemble raisins in shape and texture.

Currants
Actually a variety of small grape, these dried fruits resemble tiny raisins but have a stronger, tarter flavor. If unavailable, substitute raisins.

Dates
Sweet, deep brown fruit of the date palm tree, with a thick, sticky consistency resembling that of candied fruit. Sometimes pitted and chopped.

Figs
Compact form of the succulent black or golden summertime fruit, distinguished by a slightly crunchy texture derived from its tiny seeds. The golden Calimyrna variety has a sweet, nutty flavor that is particularly prized in baked goods.

Mango
Deep orange pieces of dried, usually sugared fruit, sold diced or in small chunks or strips.

Pears
Halved, seeded and flattened fruit, retaining the fresh pear's distinctive profile.

Prunes
Variety of dried plum, with a rich-tasting, dark and fairly moist flesh.

Raisins
Dried grapes, popular as a snack on their own. For baking, use seedless dark raisins or golden raisins (sultanas).

EGGS

Although eggs are sold in the United States in a range of standard sizes, large eggs are the most common size and should be used for the recipes in this book.

To separate an egg, crack the shell in half by tapping it against the side of a bowl and then breaking it apart with your fingers. Holding the shell halves over the bowl, gently transfer the whole yolk back and forth between them, letting the clear white drop away into the bowl. Take care not to break the yolk (the whites will not beat properly if they contain any yolk). Transfer the yolk to another bowl.

Alternatively, gently pour the egg from the shell onto the slightly cupped fingers of your clean, outstretched hand, held over a bowl. Let the whites fall between your fingers into the bowl; the whole yolk will remain in your hand.

The same basic function is also performed by an aluminum, ceramic or plastic egg separator placed over a bowl. The separator holds the yolk intact in its cuplike center while allowing the white to drip out through one or more slots in its side into the bowl.

ESPRESSO POWDER, INSTANT

Instant espresso powder or granules provides an easily blended source of intense coffee flavor to baked goods. Available in the coffee section of well-stocked food stores, in Italian delicatessens or in specialty-coffee stores.

EXTRACTS

Flavorings derived by dissolving essential oils of richly flavored foods such as **almonds** or **vanilla** in an alcohol base. Use only products labeled "pure" or "natural" extract (essence).

FLOURS

Some common types of flours used in this book include:

All-Purpose Flour

The most common flour for baking, a blend of hard and soft wheats available in all food markets. All-purpose flour is sold in its natural, pale yellow unbleached form or bleached, the result of a chemical process that not only whitens it, but also makes it easier to blend with higher percentages of fat and sugar. Bleached flour is therefore commonly used for recipes where more tender results are desired, while unbleached flour yields more crisp results. Also called plain flour.

Buckwheat Flour

Flour ground from the seeds of an herbaceous plant originating in Asia; popular in the cuisines of Russia and Eastern Europe. Its strong, earthy, slightly sour flavor is usually modulated in commercial products by the addition of a little wheat flour.

Cake Flour

Very fine-textured bleached flour for use in cakes and other baked goods. Also called soft-wheat flour. **All-purpose flour** is not an acceptable substitute.

GINGER

The rhizome of the tropical ginger plant, which yields a sweet, strong-flavored spice. Ground, dried ginger is available in the spice section of most food stores. Candied or crystallized ginger is made by first preserving pieces of ginger in sugar syrup and then coating them with granulated sugar; it is available in specialty-

NUTS

Rich and mellow in flavor, crisp and crunchy in texture, a wide variety of nuts complements holiday baking recipes. Some popular options include:

Almonds

Mellow, sweet-flavored nuts that are an important crop in California and are popular throughout the world. For baking purposes, the nuts are commonly sold already skinless (blanched) and cut into slivers or slices (flakes). Almond paste, made by finely grinding the nuts, and the sweetened form of almond paste known as **marzipan** are commonly available in the baking section of food stores.

Hazelnuts

Small, usually spherical nuts with a slightly sweet flavor. Grown in Italy, Spain and the United States. Also known as filberts. Once toasted (see instructions at right), the nuts may be stripped of their thin, papery skins by rubbing them while still warm in a folded kitchen towel.

Macadamias

Spherical nuts, about twice the diameter of **hazelnuts,** with a very rich, buttery flavor and crisp texture. Native to Australia, they are now also grown in Hawaii and Central America.

Pecans

Brown-skinned, crinkly textured nuts with a distinctive sweet, rich flavor and crisp, slightly crumbly texture. Native to the southern United States.

Pine Nuts

Small, ivory seeds extracted from the cones of a species of pine tree, with a rich, slightly resinous flavor.

Walnuts

Rich, crisp-textured nuts with crinkled surfaces. English walnuts, the most familiar variety, are grown worldwide, although California is the largest supplier. American black walnuts, sold primarily as shelled pieces, have a stronger flavor.

To Toast Nuts

Toasting brings out the full flavor and aroma of nuts. To toast any kind of nut, preheat an oven to 325°F (165°C). Spread the nuts in a single layer on a baking sheet and toast in the oven until they just begin to change color, 5–10 minutes for most nuts or about 3 minutes for pine nuts. Remove from the oven and let cool before using.

food shops or in the baking or Asian food sections of well-stocked stores.

HARD SAUCE
A thick sauce made from confectioners' (icing) sugar, butter and brandy. Often used as a topping for Christmas puddings and cakes.

MARSALA
Dry or sweet amber Italian wine from the area of Marsala, in Sicily.

MARZIPAN (SEE NUTS/ALMONDS)

MINCEMEAT, PREPARED
Old-fashioned pie or tart filling made from raisins and dried currants, apples, candied citron, sweeteners and spices. Originally, it also included finely ground (minced) beef and suet.

MOLASSES
Thick, robust-tasting, syrupy sugarcane by-product of sugar refining, a procedure that may or may not include the use of sulfur. Light molasses results from the first boiling of the syrup; dark molasses from the second boiling.

NUTMEG
Popular baking spice that is the hard pit of the fruit of the nutmeg tree. May be bought already ground or, for fresher flavor, whole. Whole nutmegs may be kept inside special nutmeg graters, which include hinged flaps that conceal a storage compartment.

POTATO STARCH
Also known as potato flour, a fine-textured flour ground from potatoes that have been cooked and dried. Sold in health-food stores and Eastern European food shops.

PUFF PASTRY
Form of pastry in which pastry dough and butter or some other solid fat are repeatedly layered to form thin leaves that puff up to flaky lightness when baked. Commercially manufactured frozen puff pastry is available in most food markets.

PUMPKIN PURÉE
The seedless orange-colored purée of pumpkin meat is available canned in most food stores.

SAFFRON
Intensely aromatic spice, golden orange in color, made from the dried stigmas of a species of crocus. Offers a delicate perfume and golden hue to baked goods. Sold either as threads—the dried stigmas—or in powdered form. Look for products labeled pure saffron.

SUGARS
Several different forms of sugar may be used in holiday baked goods:

Brown Sugar
A rich-tasting granulated sugar combined with molasses in varying quantities to yield golden, light or dark brown sugar, with crystals varying from coarse to finely granulated.

Confectioners' Sugar
Finely pulverized sugar, also known as powdered or icing sugar, which dissolves quickly and provides a thin, white decorative coating. To prevent confectioners' sugar from absorbing moisture in the air and caking, manufacturers often mix a little **cornstarch** into it.

Granulated Sugar
The standard, widely used form of pure white sugar. Do not use superfine granulated sugar unless specified in recipes.

TAPIOCA, QUICK-COOKING GRANULATED
Ground flakes of the tropical manioc (cassava) plant's dried, starchy root. Used as a dessert in itself and as a thickener for pie and tart fillings.

VANILLA BEAN
Vanilla beans are dried aromatic pods of a variety of orchid; one of the most popular flavorings in dessert making. Vanilla is most commonly used in the form of an alcohol-based extract (essence). Vanilla extract or beans from Madagascar are the best.

To split open a vanilla bean and thus expose its tiny, flavorful seeds, use a small, sharp knife to cut the bean in half lengthwise.

YEAST
One of the most widely available forms of yeast for baking, active-dry yeast is commonly sold in individual packages containing a scant 1 tablespoon (¼ oz/7 g) and found in the baking section of food stores. To save time, quick-rise yeast, which can raise breads and cakes in as little as half the normal time, is preferred in some recipes. If using fresh cake yeast, substitute ½ oz (15 g) for 1 tablespoon active dry yeast.

ZEST
Thin, brightly colored, outermost layer of a citrus fruit's peel, containing most of its aromatic essential oils—a lively source of flavor in baking. Zest may be removed using one of two easy methods:

1. Use a simple tool known as a zester, drawing its sharp-edged holes across the fruit's skin to remove the zest in thin strips. Alternatively, use a fine hand-held grater.

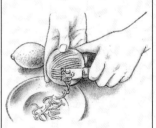

2. Holding the edge of a paring knife or vegetable peeler away from you and almost parallel to the fruit's skin, carefully cut off the zest in thin strips, taking care not to remove any of the bitter white pith with it. Then thinly slice or chop the strips on a cutting board.

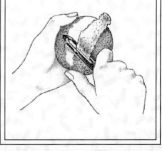

Index

ACKNOWLEDGMENTS

The publishers would like to thank the following people and organizations for
their generous assistance and support in producing this book:
Sarah Tenaglia, Kristine Kidd, Sharon C. Lott, Stephen W. Griswold, Ken DellaPenta, Claire Sanchez, Jim Obata,
Jennifer Hauser, Jennifer Mullins, and the buyers and store managers for Pottery Barn and Williams-Sonoma stores.

The following kindly lent props for the photography: Biordi Art Imports, Candelier,
Fillamento, Forrest Jones, Sue Fisher King, RH Shop and Chuck Williams.